HIGHLY PRODUTIVE TEENS WITH MAD SOCIAL SKILLS

THRIVE WITH FRIENDSHIP, HANDLE PEER PRESSURE, BULLYING, LIFE CHALLENGES, AND EVERYTHING IN BETWEEN

WILDINE PIERRE

DEDICATION

For Chris, may you always cry when we are apart
For Angel, may your flowers, hugs and affection be eternal
For all the teenagers battling the
bad days and fighting the good fight

AND FINALLY

To those who inspired it
And will not read it

"Do not go where the path may lead,
go instead where there is no path
and leave a trail".
~ **Ralph Waldo Emerson**

CONTENTS

SPECIAL BONUS

Want This Flipbook for **FREE?**

SCAN THE QR CODE

And Get FREE unlimited access to it and to all my new books samples by joining the Fan Base!

PLEASE LEAVE A REVIEW

As an independent author, reviews are my livelihood on this plat-form. SCAN THE QR CODE TO LEAVE A REVIEW ☺

PREFACE

Hello there,

Welcome! Take a deep breath, as today will be one you will remember forever. Today, your mentality, your emotions, that stellar productive teen is about to come out of that shell and shine so bright that he might be socially unrecognizable.

As you strive to discover who you are, you are bound to face obstacles, challenges, and failures; it is part of "growing up." You might be in a position where you don't know where to go or how to get there because you're simply feeling "misunderstood," you are not alone.

Being concerned about being observed, judged, socially, left out, and misunderstood are all valid feelings. However, those who set it upon themselves to overcome that fear will discover the power of their "higher self" was there all along. You will never grow up to achieve your goals or dreams without getting out of your comfort zone, socializing with others, and setting yourself apart.

You will soon understand why social skills are one of the most important and how to develop and cultivate them. We will look at various ways to set yourself up to move past the barriers you will encounter to become a teen with MAD social skills while elevating and becoming your better self.

May this book be the inspiration you need to get out of that shell and take the first step into that socialized world, but it's not a magic button. It will take time, effort, and patience to reach unsurmountable (grab a dictionary) heights. And when you conquer the world, don't forget to keep in touch. I believe in you!!!

INTRODUCTION

There are many strategies to increase social skills, which many teenagers desire. The most crucial aspect of developing these talents is the eagerness to interact with others. When deciding the right time to build your social skills, selecting the tactics that will assist you will make it a much simpler task.

Conversations are a terrific method of strengthening social skills, but this task seems nearly impossible for introverts and shy individuals. Although it's one of the most effective steps, it's often too difficult to execute. For a timid person, this may be cause enough to feel concerned and anxious; for an introvert, it may seem like an unnecessary chore.

Introverts and shy individuals are rarely expected to make such a move, and the expectations of others around them play a significant role. You may sometimes speak when no one is expecting you to. Because no one anticipates this, they may unintentionally interrupt or even disregard what you say.

The question, therefore, remains: how do you improve your social skills? You should practice with your friends and observe your conduct. Most of the time, this behavior will be natural and unforced. Therefore, attempt to learn something from it and use it to initiate talks in unfamiliar territory. The first time you engage strangers in conversation, you will realize there is nothing to fear.

You are an intriguing individual who merits the time, affection, and consideration of others. This is not a filler line but something you should understand and believe. Self-esteem plays a crucial role in developing social skills; therefore, if your self-esteem is low, work to improve it.

These are two additional considerations when attempting to improve your social skills. You must learn to listen if you genuinely want to communicate with others. Saying the words you've prepared without responding to your interlocutor's questions is a conversation-killer. It would be best if you attempted to listen to those with whom you are conversing and demonstrated an interest in what they are saying.

Conversing with others is key to improving your social skills. This GUIDE explores practical techniques to improve social skills, thrive with friendship, handle peer pressure, bullying, life challenges, and everything between.

Happy Reading

CHAPTER 1
SOCIAL SKILLS

What Are Social Skills?

Beginning at a young age, we learn the fundamentals of social skills, including how to live, interact, and get along with others. These fundamental skills, such as sharing toys and a bedroom with a brother or sister, come into play quickly if you have siblings.

These skills become even more crucial when we age and enter school as we must now share our space with more individuals. Children not adequately prepared for such an occurrence may struggle to adapt to the new society they have joined.

To define appropriate social skills, one must evaluate the environment or society in which one resides. What works in one culture may not necessarily work in another, yet basic social skills are vital for living a fulfilling life in your community, workplace, and home. Briefly, it is how we participate and conduct ourselves inside society; what is right and wrong about the society in which you reside.

Everyone is expected to conform to social norms to be accepted by society. Being impolite to others, cursing in public, and displaying disdain are negative elements of a lack of social skills. However, some prefer to go against the grain of society and lack the social skills most take lightly; we know how to behave.

Some individuals have a fundamental comprehension of this concept but are unsure how to improve their social skills in public settings. When interviewing candidates, companies evaluate their credentials and how they interact with the employer.

They seek indicators and ask questions on different themes requiring social interaction to determine if the interviewee has a solid grasp of social skills to handle delicate situations. A lack of these skills could be the difference between getting the job and not getting it; one must be able to behave correctly and with respect in the workplace and society.

A great technique to improve your social skills is to visit a public place and observe people mingling. Examine their interpersonal communication in a social context. This activity will appear ordinary until someone exhibits socially inappropriate behavior; they will act outside of social norms.

Possessing strong social skills provides you an advantage in society; people are drawn to those who exhibit appropriate social behavior and make them feel comfortable striking up a discussion. Possessing excellent social skills entails knowing how to be respectful and courteous and comprehending the norms of society. As humans, we constantly engage with one another to make these interactions the best they can be, and we must develop our social skills to their fullest potential.

A person's social skills are the specific strategies they employ to perform social functions well and, ultimately, to be socially acceptable. Your conduct and interactions with others reflect your position in the community, whether you are likely to be a friend or partner and, most crucially, whether they view you as a potential asset for a firm.

Aspects of Social Skills

Do you recall your mother instructing you to act in a certain way in social situations or in front of strangers and new acquaintances when you were a little child? You would already know how crucial it is for a person to acquire social skill development with these frequent reminders.

A person can work on three fundamental areas of social skill development. To help you appreciate the significance of developing your social skills, here are three components of social skill development and what you can do to improve them.

1. *Verbal Communication*

Being an excellent communicator is a quality many people desire, but only a select few attain. How can you not be terrified of speaking in front of a huge crowd or, even worse, on a stage because public speaking is the number one phobia of many people worldwide? Therefore, the first aspect of your social skill development you should focus on is your verbal communication ability.

If you cannot immediately attempt public speaking, you can take small steps toward your goal. Engage in casual conversation with your neighbors and other often encountered individuals. Sharing jokes or wishing them a good day will improve your daily interactions with others and your verbal communication ability.

Suppose you can communicate yourself properly without stuttering or making nervous motions. There, people will respond warmly, and you can help them feel comfortable by demonstrating your ease in social situations.

2. *Nonverbal Communication*

Nonverbal communication is an additional ability required for social skill development. Begin with your actions. When conversing with another person, you should maintain a comfortable and not too stiff posture, lean slightly towards them to indicate that you are listening and always have a ready and courteous smile. Next, you must observe the body language of the person you are conversing with. Never initiate physical contact if you believe your behavior could be misconstrued.

Consider their body language and gestures to determine their ease in your presence. A relaxed posture should indicate that the other person will engage in conversation. Last, your body language should 'agree' with the words you're speaking.

3. *Social Interaction Competencies*

To further strengthen your social skills, you must be able to recognize and resolve any potential conflicts diplomatically. If you are in a heated discussion, use diplomacy to diffuse the situation. In addition, you must determine the most appropriate behavior to adapt to the diverse personalities you will face in any social context.

By understanding these three areas of social skill development, you may manage yourself gracefully in any social context, expanding your social circle and increasing your interpersonal interactions with others.

In What Ways Are Social Skills Useful?

In one-on-one communication, listening is a two-way street, and each person aims to comprehend the messages delivered. It is a skill developed by ongoing practice. As you connect with a person, you understand their personality facets.

There are two components to social skills: verbal and nonverbal. A person with good verbal social skills knows how to say the right things at the right time, communicate freely, and keep the conversation flowing smoothly. He can use the appropriate vocal tone and quality and can convey the message in a way educated and easily understood.

A person with strong nonverbal abilities knows how and when to use body language. Your movements allow you to communicate your message through actions. Your posture, eye contact, vocal tone, and facial expression are nonverbal social skills. Excessive gestures can be overwhelming, so do not overuse them.

A person's social skills are determined by their upbringing. Our society typically influences our behavior and the social abilities of each individual vary. In some conservative cultures, a kiss and hug on the cheek as a welcoming gesture may not be socially acceptable.

Your social abilities will improve as your self-worth and self-esteem are bolstered. It is gratifying to receive appreciation from others. When help is available, one is more likely to be motivated and at ease during task completion.

Your personality is evaluated based on how you behave during encounters, how you construct your sentences, how well you adjust to your surroundings, and how you handle pressing situations. It is not enough to have a confident demeanor and a ready smile.

It is neither your appearance nor your intelligence that makes people like you. You are judged based on how others perceive you, what you do, how you do it, and who you are. Acquiring an understanding of social skills can enable you to feel welcomed and come forward to be acknowledged.

Benefits of Improving Social Skills

Do you see yourself as a "people person?"

If not, are you the opposite, content to sit in the background and wait for people to notice you?

Or do you fall in the middle?

Regardless of which of these three groups you fall into, one thing is undeniable: even on the most basic level, humans require social interaction to exist. To become less of a wallflower and more of a people person, you can do actions that will improve your social skills.

First, consider the advantages of developing social skills. You and those around you will profit from developing and improving your social skills. Suppose you are accustomed to blending in with the crowd or you dislike being the center of attention. There, you may deny yourself the chance to develop better personal relationships and meet other wonderful people outside your existing social circle.

If you can hold your own in a conversation, speak coherently in front of a large group or even on stage, and know how to make others feel at ease, then you and those around you will profit from the growth of your social skills. Not only will your self-esteem increase, but you will also feel more confident in your ability to handle yourself in any given scenario and will no longer fear making a social faux pas.

But the people around you will be drawn to your passion, self-assurance, and positive aura, increasing your chances of expanding your social circle and strengthening your relationships. You can learn about conflict management and better understand how individuals interact in social settings. By developing social skills, you can adapt to different personality types and have the confidence to fit into any circumstance.

Developing social skills includes the ability to communicate successfully, resolve problems, actively listen to what others are saying and interpret the body language of others to understand how they feel so you may construct an appropriate response. You can hold your own in any social setting with these skills.

The positive effects of developing social skills will improve your quality of life. Suppose you compare the social lives of a shy woman and a woman with a lively, contagious personality. You will notice a big difference in the number of friends they maintain.

By spending much of your time alone, you restrict your social and professional chances to those you already know. Conversely, if you learn to think positively, your outlook on life will give others the idea that you are enjoyable to be around.

Social skill development will unquestionably have a good effect on your life, given you can broaden and deepen your social connections. With the development of social skills, you will feel more confident in how you conduct yourself in social and professional settings.

Checklists

A social skills checklist is an excellent tool for monitoring your progress and determining how much your social interaction abilities have improved as you work to improve them. It summarizes the most important social skills and provides tips for understanding these talents better. This checklist is available from a counselor or social skills instructor and is available for books on communication and social etiquette.

A customizable social skills checklist can be tailored to your objectives and needs. Consider utilizing the generalized social skills checklist provided below. It can assist you in generating ideas for the social skills you wish to cultivate.

Listening is the most crucial and difficult social skill to grasp. To develop your social skills, you must be committed to achieving this goal. Self-discipline is necessary. As social skills include interpersonal communication, listening plays a significant role.

❖ *Be a good listener*

When your friend speaks, you must pay attention and vice versa. It would be best if you remembered that people want to be spoken with besides being spoken to. The social skill of listening is a give-and-take engagement. When both parties attempt to communicate with each other, this demonstrates an advanced level of social skill.

As a good listener, you should not interrupt when others are speaking. Never judge harshly and attempt to respond. Making the occasional brief remark demonstrates that you are on the same page and attentive to the topic. It requires considerable effort to be patient and respectful while waiting to be heard. However, you will learn much if you concentrate on what the other party is saying.

❖ *Always use the words "thank you" and "please."*

Using "please" and "thank you" is occasionally neglected. Most often, individuals fail to express appreciation for favors received. Take time to say "please" and "thank you" to people who have taken the time to carry out their services and you have anticipated. A decent deed earns good rewards and being kind and appreciative of their assistance will encourage them to improve their performance further.

❖ *Adopt a friendly and receptive stance.*

Your nonverbal social skills, such as body language, eye contact, and the ability to manage anxious tendencies, are essential for making others feel comfortable with you. Try to behave in a way that will not be misinterpreted as a defensive attack but rather as a welcoming gesture.

❖ *Practice chatting with and initiating discussions with strangers.*

Small talk may be tough to analyze, as little meaningful information may be provided throughout the conversation. Try asking strangers simple questions and listening to their responses. You might be amazed at how often their responses act as a springboard for an engaging discourse.

Since social skills are not definitive or material, they are difficult to measure. It would help if you had a social skills checklist while evaluating and developing your social skills.

CHAPTER 2
EFFECTIVE COMMUNICATION

What Is Effective Communication?

Effective communication is the key to a happier and healthier lifestyle as these skills are advantageous at all stages of life. These soft talents are in high demand and are essential for sustaining a comfortable and stable social life. Improving your communication skills can profoundly affect many aspects of your life and you can anticipate a boost in enjoyment, confidence, and social success.

To improve communication, it is essential to eliminate communication impediments. People often develop walls and concerns based on past communication failures and overcoming these obstacles can be difficult. Due to confidentiality concerns, a person may speak hastily or rarely make eye contact when listening. They may avoid conversations with strangers and conflicts with family members and coworkers.

Improving your communication skills might help you convey your thoughts and emotions more effectively. These improvements are beneficial in any setting, from the boardroom to the bedroom. When asked to define good communication skills, the ordinary person often overlooks the importance of listening. Listening actively and proactively is essential for effective communication, and effective communication skills comprise both speaking and listening.

Active listening is a crucial component of knowing the person or persons with whom you are interacting and enables you to connect with them more effectively. The individual's ability to empathize and sympathize with others around them is improved by effectively conveying pain, happiness, or regret.

By improving their communication skills, the individuals significantly increase their prospects for personal development. Strong communication skills can dramatically improve one's leadership qualities, including the ability to motivate subordinates at work or family members at home.

Effective communication skills are an essential component of personal stress management from the standpoint of self-maintenance. By improving communication skills, a person can become more assertive, having a greater capacity to take control of a conversation or circumstance and achieve the desired outcome. Improved communication skills can also significantly improve a person's ability to execute conflict management at home and work.

Improved conversational abilities will boost a person's potential to make new friends; talking effectively enables a person to project a more confident, charismatic, and friendly personality. These improvements in personal development will also improve the individual's networking abilities.

Good networking is increasingly vital to success in today's global, competitive, and fast-paced employment market. The capacity to "schmooze" with top management or ingratiate oneself with company officials can increase responsibility, compensation, and promotion prospects.

Fidgeting hand movements and eye movements are obstructions to communication. Many consider it the most difficult component to monitor and improve. People often concentrate so hard on what they are saying or hearing they are unaware of their physical actions.

Mastering the skill of public speaking is challenging for the typical person and it requires a delicate balance to convey a vital point to an audience while retaining their interest. An effective communicator can find a method to bring his speech to life by utilizing his vocal strength and his physical power to entertain and educate his audience.

Understanding the individual or group you are communicating with is crucial to good communication. A strong communicator must determine when certain jokes or certain behaviors are suitable and when they are not. Humor may be a potent ally, but it can swiftly turn against you if used irresponsibly.

The ability to effectively employ the written word is a crucial element of effective communication skills. Many realize that, despite their education and degrees, their writing skills leave much to be desired. As with many things in life, the growth of writing abilities must be tackled in little steps with the aid of training. Try writing simply about your likes and dislikes or a brief apology to someone as practice. Successful writing is conveying a point through emotive and polished language without 'offending' the reader's sensibilities with a lengthy speech that does little to promote comprehension.

The Value of Effective Communication

We connect with different people daily, but are we communicating effectively? Do individuals listen to you, or do they hear your words? But authentic listening demands undivided attention and a reply. When people merely hear your words, you typically receive no acknowledgment of what was said, the message, or its significance.

Communication is exchanging or transmitting ideas, beliefs, or data through speech, writing, signs, and symbols. Words alone can make people happy, sad, glad, or angry, and they might attract or repel others and inspire or anger them.

The spoken word is the most popular form of communication, but there are others, including recordings, letters, symbols, graphs, and images. A sage once remarked, "A picture is worth a thousand words."

Communication is possibly the most important aspect of effective human connections, and effective communication is the art of understanding and being understood by others. Often, achieving one's objectives means working with and through others. To do so, we must exchange ideas, thoughts, opinions, and other forms of information.

There are more means of communication, such as gestures, facial expressions, and tone of voice. To be effective, all communication must take place in a two-way situation. One person transmits the message, which is received by another, who sends one or more messages in response. One-way, authoritarian communication is always less effective than two-way communication.

Objectives of Effective Communication

When we communicate, we anticipate an outcome. We evolved the ability to communicate with others for the following reasons: to provide and receive information; to stimulate thought; to negotiate and persuade; to build a better understanding; to make suggestions and give orders.

When the message is not delivered effectively, the audience does not comprehend what we aim to convey. Ineffective communication can result in numerous problems, such as not enough information being provided or the information provided being inaccurate. The information is given too quickly; listeners jump to conclusions and interpret a vague message; its meaning is not explicit or precise; people are afraid to ask questions.

To become a better and more effective communicator, you will need to master these abilities and techniques: take notes; be prepared; plan; offer detailed commands or instructions; to ensure you are understood, ask the listener(s) questions.

Take your time and slow down your speech; use visual assistance, if appropriate:

❖ **Utilize pace, modulation, and accent.**

❖ **Summarize the content covered.**

❖ **Recapitulate and be specific.**

❖ **Pose questions.**

We have all witnessed and heard exceptional communicators and speeches. There have been significant phrases from remarkable speeches and excellent communicators that have endured throughout history.

Example: "Ask not what your country can do for you but what you can do for your country," "I have a dream," "We have nothing to fear but fear itself."

Why do we recall important phrases and words employed by outstanding communicators so well? What they said, how they said it and what it meant to us when we heard it are among the many reasons.

When you have learned the abilities and tactics of good communication, the same can be said of you. Yes, practice is required, and the skills and procedures are identical whether speaking to one hundred people or one person.

Learning to become a more effective communicator requires the mastery of additional principles, skills, and strategies.

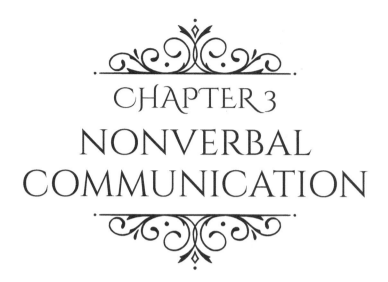

CHAPTER 3
NONVERBAL COMMUNICATION

What Is Nonverbal Communication?

Nonverbal expressions and communication are becoming one of the world's fastest-growing modes of interpersonal communication. Hundreds of types of nonverbal communication are known to modern civilization, all used in interpersonal contact.

Physical and written communication will be examined within the confines of this book. Within these two frameworks of nonverbal communication are many nonverbal entities or variations because people communicate on different levels.

Nonverbal communication includes facial expressions such as a smile, a smirk, and even wrinkles. Eye contact or eye avoidance, comparable to rolling the eyes or not looking at the person speaking or directly at someone, gives a sense of disdain.

Also, body posture, hand and foot movements, and other body movements and positions might be interpreted as nonverbal communication. Similar to the customs of ethnic dances, looks and posture convey something. If you listen intently with your eyes and not your ears, you will notice that every movement gives some nonverbal expression.

Body language, gestures, and signals can be unnoticeable or noticeable forms of nonverbal communication. There are many cross-cultural variances in nonverbal communication, particularly about body language, gestures, facial expressions, touch, posture, and eye contact. The breach of one's personal space can be conveyed through nonverbal gestures.

Retreating from another person conveys the idea that the individual is too close for comfort. Nonverbal communication might be interpreted differently based on the culture with which one is most familiar. Verbal communication is not the only mode of communication we employ.

Often, we typically view communication as the sending and receiving of nonverbal messages between two or more parties. Occasionally, these wordless signals can be delivered unconsciously and without the intention of being seen by the recipient.

Because men and women differ in how they transmit and receive nonverbal messages, it is reasonable to assume that women are more adept at this activity than males and can convey their intended message with great skill. Some males have become adept at interpreting body language, concluding that both the use and comprehension of body language are special social tools.

How Verbal and Nonverbal Communication Affect Relationships

Communication is the fuel that powers friendships. How can you come to an understanding in an argument if you do not communicate? Whatever works for you will be beneficial to your friendship. Always remember there are two modes of communication: spoken and nonverbal. These are most called verbal and nonverbal communication.

Verbal Interaction

You share your ideas and opinions whenever you talk to someone through spoken words. This is a great asset and the foundation of a strong friendship. Spoken language will allow your friend to comprehend your true intent. Also, it can remedy problems if they arise. Since you have an open line of communication, your connection can flourish.

The suppression of emotions can prevent vocal communication., and this can result in uncomfortable feelings. Remember to communicate your thoughts. Never be overly harsh, but always tell the truth. You can understand each other better when you're angry than when you're calm.

Nonverbal Interaction

This represents all other nonverbal content. It will be evident in your attitudes and movements. Always "read between the lines" when attempting to comprehend your friend's genuine emotions. Observe how your friend reacts to different situations. This can help you grasp simple things such as their preferences

Body language reveals an individual's personality. With this information, you can discern specific underlying characteristics you wouldn't otherwise know because they don't express them.

Communication, both verbal and nonverbal, can affect a friendship on multiple levels. For instance, you can resolve conflicts and develop closer bonds through conversation. If you observe the other person's body language, you can preempt arguments and obtain the upper hand.

How to Easily Read Body Language

As a form of communication, we pay little attention to body language. Often, others "hear" something from our body and how we use it we were not even aware we were "speaking," and it can come back to haunt us!

According to experts, up to fifty percent of our communication is delivered nonverbally or via actions rather than words. That is somewhat more than most of us may have anticipated! Learning to read body language can aid comprehension of what someone is saying. Mastering the use of it can help you convey your point more effectively than words alone.

What Am I Referring to When I Combine the Words Body and Language?

This language is a sort of nonverbal, body-based communication, which could be a facial expression or a posture. Many people, for instance, speak actively, utilizing their bodies to convey their views. Many "hand talkers" constantly use their hands to share information, highlight a point or keep a story moving forward.

Posture alone can convey a certain mood through body language.

* Sagging shoulders, a rounded back, and a drooping head may imply sadness or shyness.

* A brisk walk with the chest puffed out, shoulders elevated, and head held high may convey confidence or arrogance. When a person's arms are folded across the chest, this is typically interpreted as a standoffish or an unpleasant pose.

It is remarkable how much can be gleaned through body language! Not only can you utilize your body to gauge a person's attitude or mood, but you may also gain a deeper understanding of interpersonal connections. These nonverbal indicators can indicate attachment between individuals.

Body language can be divided down into general categories that recur often.

General Categories

1. *Aggressive. Aggressive behavior is inherently scary.*

2. *Attentive. This style of body language indicates engagement and interest.*

3. *Bored. Exhibited by yawning and a lack of eye contact or other visual listening signs, this is the antithesis of attentiveness.*

4. *Concluded. This isolates you from others. Crossed arms and a distant stance are common indicators of restricted communication.*

5. *Deception. When attempting to get away with a falsehood, deception is often employed. It is characterized by anxious conduct triggered by guilt and anxiety.*

6. *Defensive. This body language is typically observed when someone is guarding information or his inner thoughts.*

7. *Dominant. Those who enjoy being in charge exhibit domineering body language. Dominant people typically stand tall with their chests thrust out.*

8. *Emotions. Sentiment dramatically influences conversations. It fluctuates regularly with mood.*

9. *Evaluation. Body language evaluation is utilized when deciding or hesitating to make a judgment.*

10. *Greeting. This body language is employed when interacting with somebody for the first time.*

11. *Open. Open body language is hospitable and pleasant.*

12. *Prepared for action. This style of body language indicates readiness and willingness.*

13. *Relaxed and content. Relaxed body language is exhibited by individuals at ease, content, and tranquil.*

14. *Passionate. Romantic body language is flirtatious and communicates attraction.*

15. *Submissive. This demonstrates your yielding nature.*

These are the most prevalent thoughts conveyed by a stance, pose combo, or posture. Many bodily positions have diverse connotations based on the individual, the context, and the observer's culture.

For instance, in the United States, it is courteous to stare intermittently into another person's eyes to indicate that you are listening to them. It is considered rude in Japan. In the United States, it is normal for people to smile at one another as a sign of friendship. However, in Korea, grins are signs of embarrassment and are not expressed in public.

It is best, when traveling overseas, to behave as the Romans do, to adopt the culture of the country you are visiting so you may effectively communicate your views.

Being more mindful of your body language when conversing with others is crucial! These body language guidelines will improve your knowledge and communication abilities, paving the way for more productive interactions with others.

CHAPTER 4
ACTIVE LISTENING

What Is Active Listening?

Active listening is a term that may be considered a trendy buzzword in certain areas today. What does it mean precisely, and why should anyone care?

Active listening is a strategy that can improve overall communication, acquire a clearer grasp of a speaker's message, and make a speaker feel heard. People have a strong need to be heard.

Some argue that the need to be heard is one of our fundamental human wants since it easily translates into a sense of acceptance, acknowledgment and belonging. These emotions have been the focus of psychological writing on fundamental human needs.

When one person speaks to another, he or she expects the other to listen. This expectation is heightened during times of conflict. How many of you were having lunch with a friend or coworker when the other person answered a phone call or checked his or her Facebook page?

How do you feel when attempting to communicate with someone who looks more interested in sending a text message or browsing the internet?

I will hazard a guess and say it likely does not feel pleasant. Why? Because the other individual is not listening. Perhaps he/she hears you, but he/she is not genuinely listening. When this occurs, you may feel less valuable than a text message or the most recent Tweet. You may experience rudeness or a lack of recognition.

So, what would happen if this someone did the exact opposite and gave you his/her undivided attention when you spoke? Your negative feelings of "he/she is not listening to me" or "I suppose I am not as important as his/her phone" could be converted into feelings of acceptance, acknowledgment and belonging.

When someone sincerely listens, he or she will give you his or her undivided attention. With a few exceptions, their attention will not be diverted from you and your message by a ringing phone or a text message. Active listening can be transformative.

To actively listen, the listener must devote one hundred percent of his or her attention to the speaker and the message. There is no room for irrelevant ideas such as what you will have for lunch or debating which of the Avengers is the strongest.

Why? Because active listening requires participation in the communication. He/she is an active participant, not just an observer. Consider the following illustration.

Sally conflicts with her mother, Judy. Sally believes her mother rarely listens to her. Sally recently asked her mother not to discuss the job she didn't get. Judy indicated to Sally she understood by nodding her head.

Two minutes later, Judy initiates a discussion with a neighbor and explains that her daughter didn't get the job. Sally cries and rages at her mother, "You never listen to me. Why do I bother communicating with you?"

Judy would not have just nodded her head in response to Sally's plea to refrain from discussing the job in question if she had engaged in active listening. Instead, she may have responded, "It appears that you are saying it embarrasses you when I discuss your personal life with others. Is that correct?"

What did Judy do differently because of her active listening?

She interpreted Sally's message and relayed it in her own terms. Finally, Judy asked, "Is that correct?" to confirm that she had grasped the information correctly.

Try active listening the next time you find yourself in a conversation with someone. Try repeating what the other person said using your own words and confirm your understanding by asking them whether you've understood correctly. Active listening is likely to help you become a better communicator rapidly. Test it out!

Effective Considerations for Active Listening

Most teens do not listen when someone is speaking passionately. Mastering the art of listening is a prerequisite for leadership in the workplace. *Follow the concepts below to become an engaged and effective listener.*

1. Always practice listening to people without focusing on the barriers to listening around you. Listen to folks by observing their facial expressions. Try to comprehend their feelings.

2. Always concentrate on one person when listening. Do not attempt to listen to two or three individuals at once.

3. Concentrate intently when you're listening to music. This will improve your ability to concentrate while listening to others.

4. Practice taking notes to improve your comprehension and concentration when listening to a lecture or seminar.

5. Active listening will aid in problem resolution. Always pay close attention to the information being given to you when listening.

6. When listening to a foreign language, try to comprehend the tone and spirit of the content.

7. Always attempt to comprehend the problem from the perspective of others.

8. If you are experiencing similar circumstances, do not overreact and overwhelm the speaker with your experiences and recommendations.

9. Always nod and mirror the same facial expressions as the speaker when listening to others.

10. Always attempt to paraphrase material when they pause.

11. Do not inquire about the speaker's IQ level and refrain from asking for additional information.

12. You must react with the same voice, tone and timbre as the speaker. If the speaker is excited about his subject, the audience is expected to feel the same way. They should not see the speaker with a sad disposition.

13. Whatever the conversation's outcome, expressing satisfaction will improve relations and comprehension. You must always guarantee your participation in future debates.

14. Do not assume that the speaker is awaiting your response simply because he is speaking to you. Wait until he solicits your opinion.

15. You should not criticize while someone is speaking. You shouldn't belittle the emotions of others.

16. Active listening will foster a polite environment.

17. If you are uninterested in the conversation, strive to postpone it and refrain from participating.

18. Always attempt to grasp the substance of the content.

19. Avoid responding while others are still speaking. You may miss important details.

20. While speaking, stand in front of the listener. Avoid folding your hands and displaying awkward body language when conversing with strangers.

CHAPTER 5
CONFLICT RESOLUTION

What Is a Conflict?

Before we can deal with conflict effectively, we need to understand whether it is a conflict or just what we call undesired reality. In contrast to conflict, the unpleasant reality is unlikely to alter or, if it changes, requires a lot of leadership or management time and effort.

Change is possible but unlikely to occur in the foreseeable future. Thus, it is merely an unwelcome fact and dealing with an unpleasant reality differs from dealing with confrontation.

Throughout our lives, we make hierarchical choices. Each decision, at each level of the hierarchy, comes with restrictions, limitations, and certain givens that are undesired realities.

Then how do you cope with unwelcome reality?

You accept it. Unless you will champion the cause of changing someone, you must accept the unpleasant reality and focus your efforts on things you can influence or alter.

When people do this, there is a tremendous sense of liberation, an increase in energy, and a stronger capacity for dispute resolution.

The causes are twofold:

1. People are not demoralized by their recurrent failure to change what they perceive as conflict but as an unwelcome reality

2. There is a greater emphasis on what can be changed or resolved, i.e., actual conflict.

What is the nature of conflict?

Conflict makes you feel threatened because your ideas, beliefs, or points of view are being contested (typically by another person or persons). Fear lies at the heart of all threats and this apprehension establishes the two usual responses to conflict:

Actively attempt to resolve the disagreement or withdraw from the conflict, hoping it will resolve itself or disappear. This results from our internal psychology.

When we perceive a threat, our natural response is to fight or flee. The strength of the response is proportional to the perceived severity of the threat. The "fight" response entails attacking any perceived threat or conflict with aggression and attempting to resolve it in any way possible. The "flight" response is to flee the dispute and ignore it until it presumably no longer exists.

Intensity varies among conflicts.

A minor conflict occurs when two people have different objectives, views, ideas, or desires. This category encompasses two individuals in negotiations. Each party will seek a favorable conclusion without necessarily desiring the other party's defeat but wanting the satisfaction of their own needs and desires. Even two good ideas can be a conflict situation.

These contradictory notions are fundamentally dangerous. If heeded, one concept will jeopardize the other idea's existence. At the other extreme of conflict, intensity seeks to eliminate the other side's perspective and people.

However, conflict is not inevitably negative. Conflict might generate fresh ideas or heightened awareness of the topic at hand. Conflict can unite people and therefore is not inherently harmful. How we respond to conflict determines the positive or negative outcomes. Thus, how we resolve disputes has long-lasting impacts.

Baggage Can Increase Conflict

The consequences of conflict resolution last for a long time, which is one of its magical properties. Even if a person has done a million things perfectly, a single mishandled quarrel might have a greater impact than all the "good things." Better trust and a more solid foundation for conflict resolution the next time around are the benefits of correctly managing conflict.

Resolving conflicts by leading individuals through an emotional process of forgiving and noting that each new experience will be treated as a separate entity rather than an extension of the past, could be the key to resolving conflicts. Confrontation is difficult when you're carrying around a lot of stuff and your hands are already full.

Practical Steps for Resolving Conflicts

Therefore, if we have distinguished between unpleasant reality and actual conflict, if we understand what conflict is, and we have buried our baggage, we may proceed to conflict resolution. However, remember that conflict resolution is only a portion of conflict management.

The true power of conflict resolution can be unlocked by grasping the broader picture. If you follow a basic six-step strategy with patience and do not seek solutions prematurely, you can miraculously achieve win-win outcomes.

First, defuse emotion to prepare for the genuine issue.

Most of the time, we will experience emotion in conflict situations. Our objective is not to eliminate feelings but to govern our emotions, so they do not control us.

How do you control your emotions?

How can you prevent emotions from being the driving factor during a conflict?

Rarely does someone enter a dispute with you and say, "Listen, I'm in conflict with you and I'm the problem." Instead, they say, "You're the problem," and they say it with considerable emotion. With dispute resolution, rarely is there an issue-driven, solution-focused procedure. Instead, it is a self-protective, blame-driven process.

The most significant component of this mutual protective stance is the emotion the other person feel. Objectivity is one of your most prominent friends in conflict resolution, and your worst opponent is narcissistic defense. Emotion can diminish objectivity and heighten defensiveness. Emotions are the driving force behind unsuccessful conflict resolution.

How do you control emotion?

We must equal their intensity to influence another person's emotions and convey the message, "I hear you. I understand what you mean by that, and I'm eager to work with you on it!"

These are the two things people want to hear while in disagreement with us: we are listening to them and are eager to do something about their situation. However, our natural default mode is to defend our "self." This is normal because of the perceived threat at the heart of the dispute and our natural defenses rise.

This self-preservation reflex encourages the other person to protect themselves, creating a dispute against each other rather than a conflict over an idea or problem. Controlling one's emotions is the first step in shifting the focus from accusing each other to identifying the genuine conflict issue.

The other person's emotions can be managed using meaningful sentences expressed with sincerity. "I can see your point," "I understand you feel this way," or "I can imagine myself feeling that way too" are effective ways to convey understanding authentically.

This acceptance and comprehension decrease the other individual's emotions. If the other person is too emotionally charged to communicate, you must withdraw and offer to discuss the issue later.

We can employ different approaches to control our emotions to identify the underlying problem behind the dispute.

Step One:

Take a break

Putting distance and time between yourself and the subject helps restore objectivity and reduce emotion. Another approach is to consciously set aside the need to defend oneself and search for and concentrate on the main issue behind the other person's frustrating communication.

Changing our perspective is the most effective psychological approach for controlling our emotions. It is relatively simple, and it may not appear to have the ability to influence our feelings. However, we have received many accounts of this basic tool's efficacy.

When you are in the present reacting to the other person and the scenario from where you stand, conditioned responses within you will lead your emotions to rise. When we shift that perspective, the same conditioned responses don't occur.

Here is precisely what I mean: Imagine observing yourself conversing with the opposing party. Imagine what it would look like to watch yourself in this encounter from across the room.

This simple shift in viewpoint will provide you with a more objective stance. You can attempt it as you read this sentence. Imagine seeing yourself reading these words. Notice how your perspective shifts. When you feel emotionally charged, your emotions shift and become more objective.

Prepare for the situation by diffusing the emotion. Typically, emotional concerns obscure the underlying problem. Reacting emotionally will hinder our ability to address the real issue. We can exacerbate the problem by responding to an emotionally charged individual with further emotion.

Step Two:

Listen and accept the individual's perceived problem

Acceptance is distinct from agreement. We may disagree with the person's position on the problem; however, if we do not accept it, the individual feels forced to continue discussing their concern until they are persuaded that we have heard and accepted it.

Once the emotion is under control, it is essential to continue asking clarifying questions with a genuine desire to comprehend the main issue this individual is discussing.

You must comprehend before proceeding to the next phase or resolving the problem. "Seek to understand before attempting to be understood," says Stephen Covey. This is the next step in our conflict management method.

There is a slight but significant distinction between "I agree with your concern" and "I agree with your concern." You can agree this individual has a problem and agree on their concern, but you do not have to share the concern. To effectively manage conflicts, a person must realize that we embrace and comprehend them, which is adequate.

How is this done?

Do not discuss your opinion or perspective until you have reached step three. Do not justify or defend yourself and do not explain your perspective or comprehension. Listen and clarify until you've heard what they must say.

You do this by repeating the sentence, "What I'm hearing you say is 'X' and your fundamental issue is 'Y,' is that it? Do I understand your position and worry completely?" till they consent. Then and only then may you go to the third stage.

By now, the person should be interested, calm, and ready to hear what you offer. They are in that position because you demonstrated genuine concern by listening to them without emotional defensiveness. Here is where the magic begins.

If you don't execute steps one and two, you have usually perpetuated a dispute, the dynamics of which are controlled by the seriousness of the problem and the emotional ownership of the individual in conflict with you.

When you complete steps one and two in their entirety, the other person will be prepared to listen to you. Once you have received confirmation, you comprehend their position, restate your acceptance of it, thank them for their openness, and reiterate your readiness to collaborate with them toward a resolution. This prepares the way for the third step.

Step Three:

Obtain permission before speaking your mind

Say something like, "Now that I've considered and acknowledged your problems, issues, and opinions, may I share mine? I realize that your ideas differ from mine, and I do not assert that mine are correct, but if we want to work together to find a solution, I must also voice my concerns. Do you agree?"

If the individual agrees, you can express your thoughts, viewpoints, reasons, feelings, and understandings. If the person says no, you need to review step two or you are at an impasse and require some mediation, facilitation, or arbitration.

A basic rule of conflict management is this; don't go where the other person isn't. If their emotions flare up again, return to defusing them. If they continue to insist on speaking, you must return to step two. Conflict cannot be resolved until both parties are on the same page. It is a rule of dispute resolution, and it is a life guideline.

When expressing your thoughts, do so in an impartial, non-threatening, and non-judgmental manner. Avoid trying to defend yourself. Keep to the point. Documenting the other person's primary issue and concern is a good tool for maintaining both parties' neutrality. You can then record your own.

This gives them both equal importance in the discussion. If the person fights with your remarks, remind them gently that you heard them and that you'd prefer it if you could also express yourself.

These words may be helpful: "I appreciate your willingness to assist in resolving this situation, but I believe it would be beneficial for both of us to hear my issues and concerns. Your problem was 'X,' and your worry was 'Y.' I would like to hear your response after I have shared mine." Step three is expressing your thoughts completely, preparing you for the fourth step.

Step Four:

Solicit agreement on your issues and concerns

After you have spoken, confirm that the recipient has heard your entire message. Say something like, "Now that I've shared my thoughts, do you agree that these are my worries and concerns, even though they differ from yours?"

If they do not, ask which portion they do not comprehend. Remind them you are not attempting to convince them of your opinions, but you're stating them with the purpose of both of you knowing all the perspectives, issues, and concerns.

Making the other person understand that they should do nothing other than listen and acknowledge that you have these issues and concerns facilitates their acceptance of your problems as your issues. Here is when true magic occurs.

We are attempting to resolve this. We have stated that conflict management is a component and cannot exist independently. Step five will occur if you have followed steps one through four with sincerity and thoroughness.

Step Five:

Work together toward a resolution

When both parties in a conflict genuinely comprehend each other's perspectives, issues, and worries, there is a readiness to collaborate toward a win-win resolution. To begin step five, you establish clarity and comprehension by reviewing the issues and concerns of both sides.

Next, you ask the other person if they are prepared to engage in some possible thinking with you so you can both achieve your goals. This focuses your energy on a good direction, allowing you to work as a team.

Before completing step five, it is sometimes prudent to take a break. You may need to collect further data or if you have reached a stalemate, you may need to enlist the assistance of other parties or seek the intervention of a mediator, facilitator, or arbitrator.

Sometimes, allowing time to pass before pursuing a solution might result in better objectivity, fewer emotions, and more inventiveness in pursuing a win-win resolution. Remain in step five to work with whatever assistance is necessary and to continue collaborating toward a mutually acceptable solution.

Step Six:

Close and consent to release

Most of the time, the dynamics of earlier conflict episodes heavily influence the current conflict. How a previous conflict was resolved typically controls the beginning of the dynamics for the subsequent conflict.

The emotions and issues resulting from past partially resolved or unresolved conflict resolutions are stored and released during the following conflict episode. It is therefore crucial that you agree to resolve the current conflict issue and let it go as you move forward.

Occasionally, this is easier to say than to execute. But if two parties can agree on a resolution and closure, it is easier to let go of the dynamics of this present episode and not accumulate baggage.

To remember our most straightforward conflict management system, remember the four Cs:

❖ Control your emotions (practice self-control)

❖ Clarify concerns

◈   Create alternatives

◈   Choose and let go

Conflict cannot be avoided. When you uncover the worry behind the disagreement, the person competing with you becomes your ally, working with you toward the larger good. Keep your emotions in check, uncover the main concern behind the argument, and utilize it as a learning opportunity to reach a win-win for both people.

These six actions can help you be most effective in resolving a conflict: Defuse emotion, listen and accept, obtain permission and speak, solicit agreement, work toward a settlement, close, and agree to let go.

Conflict is a natural element of life and nearly every relationship. People have diverse beliefs, objectives, needs, and desires, so disagreement is inevitable when they attempt to work or live together. While some people view conflict as a bad thing, in reality, having different opinions is a good thing. When those opinions conflict, it can be an important opportunity to find a compromise or explore new and better ways of doing things.

However, conflicts become a problem when they do not lead to productive dialogue or successful solutions. When people grow upset due to a problem, use hurtful language, or shut off debate, this can harm a relationship and make it difficult to resolve the conflict constructively. To resolve a quarrel, withdrawing, giving in with resentment, or pushing your opinion on others can also be detrimental.

It is prudent to acquire conflict resolution skills to avoid escalating a conflict into a problem. You can learn how to handle any disagreement more constructively and how to diffuse or prevent arguments with training in conflict resolution.

With the assistance of conflict resolution training, a quarrel does not need to become an argument but rather an opportunity to build a relationship by collaborating to find an effective resolution.

CHAPTER 6
EMPATHY

What Is Empathy?

We describe empathy as the capacity to perceive the emotions of others and to determine what they may think and experience. Most commonly, empathy is described using the metaphors "putting oneself in another's shoes" or "seeing the world through another's eyes." It promotes an emotional connection and involvement between lovers, family, friends, and strangers.

Empathy is an essential component of emotions and a distinct emotion characterized by a felt element of connection and a bodily response to spoken or nonverbal communication. It pertains to closeness and an awareness of what another individual is experiencing. Some persons are naturally more empathic than others, while others may find it difficult to relate. What causes empathy and why some people are more empathic than others are among the topics that psychology seeks to answer.

In each leadership position, including political and social leadership, leaders must empathize with the other group members to influence the ideas and decisions of their followers.

Teachers must also empathize with their pupils as this builds a bond without which the teaching experience is pointless for both students and teachers. Empathy is the ability to motivate or influence another individual by tapping into their emotions.

Psychologically speaking, humans have four fundamental types of empathy: self-empathy, mirror (emotional) empathy, cognitive empathy, and compassionate empathy.

❖ *Self-empathy* is offering oneself empathy, listening with compassion, and understanding one's feelings and unmet needs. This does not miraculously solve our issues or fulfill all our demands.

However, it assists us in feeling connected and grounded inside ourselves. It can also help us express ourselves with more candor. Though it may not solve issues, it makes them easier to tolerate.

❖ *Emotional empathy* entails experiencing the other person's feelings as if they were contagious. It makes one sensitive to the emotional world of others, which is advantageous in different professions. There is a disadvantage associated with emotional empathy, which happens when individuals cannot manage their emotions.

This is psychological tiredness leading to professional burnout, a regular occurrence. Those in the medical field can avoid burnout by cultivating a deliberate disconnection. However, when detachment turns into indifference, it can severely impair professional care.

❖ *Cognitive empathy* entails understanding the other person's emotions and potential thoughts, which is instrumental in negotiations and motivation. Cognitively empathetic persons (also known as perspective takers) are influential leaders and managers because they can motivate others to offer their best effort.

However, there can be disadvantages to this empathy. If the narcissists, Machiavellians, and psychopaths—have a high level of cognitive empathy, they can torture others to the point of exploitation. These individuals have little compassion for their victims and are adept at calibrating their cruelty.

❖ *Compassionate empathy*—also known as empathetic care— involves comprehending a person's plight and feeling with them and acting spontaneously to assist them if necessary. In actuality, the empathetic concern is the essential component of an empathic reaction in a specific circumstance and is the characteristic most required of social volunteers.

Empathy is a fundamental trait

Humans are endowed with diverse degrees of innate empathy; hence, our responses to the plight of others vary. It is one of the most fundamental human characteristics, so much so we perceive those who lack it as dangerous or mentally ill.

Typically, females score higher than males on typical empathy, social sensitivity, and emotion detection tests. Its inherent nature can be demonstrated by seeing how young toddlers react to the feelings of family members. When family members are in difficulty, not only do youngsters display concern but so do some household pets.

The pets hover close by and rest their heads on their owners' laps, demonstrating that even animals are empathetic. Besides humans, many other species show empathy to varying degrees.

Research provides solid evidence for empathy in animals. In 1964, the *American Journal of Psychiatry* reported that rhesus monkeys refused to pull a chain that delivered food to themselves if doing so shocked a buddy. After observing another monkey suffer a shock, a monkey stopped dragging the chain for twelve days. These primates essentially starved themselves to prevent harming other creatures. Amazing, isn't it?

The Phases of Empathy

A person's ability to anticipate another person's emotional re-actions is the culmination of their empathy, which begins with intuition. *Below are the phases of empathy:*

1. Instinct

2. Connection

3. Deliberation

4. Anticipation

5. Inspiration

The first step of empathy is to be naturally aware of the other person's feelings and sensations or thought processes, which establishes the second stage of empathy or a sense of connection.

When two people are connected, they anticipate each other's reactions and develop a sense of mutual consideration. Empathy can be one-sided in many situations, but it can also be reciprocal in others, such as a relationship between a patient and her therapist.

An empathic person may foresee the emotional responses of the other after the connection has been created, and there is a deep sense of consideration and understanding of why the other is feeling a specific way. Having the ability to put yourself in another person's shoes means being able to read their body language and respond accordingly.

When a teacher or therapist needs to motivate or influence another person, they have reached the highest level of empathy where they can empathize with them on a more directive level. It's possible that empathy was developed to exert influence on the other person to achieve specific objectives.

With empathy, you're attempting to uplift and enthuse the other person, and empathy entails this as a necessary component.

Depending on the context in which the empathy is expressed, feelings of love and admiration can occur. It all relies on the empathy you've developed. From a psychological perspective, empathy involves providing for the safety, security, and feelings of love and belonging of another person or group because you anticipate that is probably where their needs lie.

People's desire for love, attachment, and belongingness (psychological needs) lies in the middle of their need for safety and security. Empathy is a universal human need, manifested in its giving and receiving.

Individuals satisfy their love and belongingness needs through relationships with others, and empathy provides safety and security through love and belongingness. Thus, the purpose of empathy, as described by Maslow's hierarchy of needs theory, is to make the other person happy by offering a sense of security and support, thus inspirational.

Empathy improves social interaction because it provides familiarity, connectivity, and consideration between individuals and helps teach and preserve human ideals.

The Influence of Empathy

Sometimes, your life may appear to be excellent or even unique to others, but that is until you face options that are not as obvious as they may seem. You want to reach out to discover a kind hand, one reaching back, offering advice, leading you, assisting you or at the very least demonstrating compassion.

One thing is sure: It is never inappropriate to ask for assistance, solicit another person's viewpoint or at least evaluate the input of another person's experience. Seeking the attention or aid of someone who may have more life experience than you or me could be of fantastic support or incredible service!

We are all placed in the world to deliver a gift or service, first to ourselves, by having pride in our talent, work ethic, or ability to be original or creative, then to serve humanity by any means that come to us naturally. Ways of service may arise due to a trait, discipline, or ability we have been taught or that we have intrinsically or organically developed. Some of the most extraordinary skills exhibited by people originate within their minds.

Consider, for instance, the qualities of kindness, compassion, and yes, even empathy, which are all excellent to possess! Did you know empathy is not as natural for some individuals as one might assume?

Empathy is a feeling of compassion for your fellow human, animal, or anything or anyone in our magnificent world. We engage others with empathy and demonstrating love and kindness to all people and things. Understanding the power of empathy unlocks so many doors for you, me, and others in our sphere of influence! Empathy is a universal and lofty calling that provides understanding, beneficial acts of kindness, or sheer comfort to an otherwise uncomfortable life, circumstance, or frightening condition.

Empathy is a considerably superior trait to exhibit than covetousness, fear, judgment, or envy. It will provide comprehension, help you reconcile conflicting points of view, or even give you greater patience when confronted with impracticable situations.

Occasionally, we find ourselves in situations for which there is no rhyme or explanation. Even if no one else would, it is best to show yourself compassion. Even if someone or a group of individuals deny giving you misery or disgust, you must maintain mental peace.

A little advice!

Planting and planning in productive ways make this trying period ripe for resolution and solutions. Realize what is happening, repurpose your thoughts and align with your mind; it is now the greatest moment to focus on another channel.

Learn to thrive despite your suffering and see your life, attention, and energy transform. Change in one's life might occur in novel and even better ways! BE CONSCIOUS that the worst days are behind you and the best days are ahead of you. Allow that to permeate your mind and accept it as your truth. Concentrate on someone other than you.

When assisting others, especially those who must land securely after a fall, you can demonstrate empathy by helping them land with both feet on the ground. After they have suffered emotional distress or unresolved conflict, surround them with comfort.

Suffering through adversity is not a simple task, something that you and I understand, especially if you are sensitive and feel the agony and suffering of others and your own. As sure as the existence of our oceans and waves is in our lives, the struggle can be analyzed but can never be eliminated.

When your life is at a crossroads and you cannot decide whether to turn left or right, don't move at all!

OH NO! This is the optimal moment to contemplate your decision and seek inner guidance. Perhaps prayer, meditation, quiet time alone, or deep introspection are outdated for some. Still, for some of us, they seem to function best in combination, with any two or all three working exceptionally well.

**Never undervalue or be opposed to showing or experiencing empathy for another person. One day, that same empathic support and energy will return to you and potentially be the glue that holds you or puts you back together again.

Importance of Empathy in Life

❖ Empathy plays a significant role in almost every aspect of our lives. Although empathy is a trait we inherit, it is also a talent that can be developed and plays a big part in our performance in these fields.

The role of empathy in an individual's life depends on how that individual conceptualizes it, which varies considerably. However, empathy reflects what has been experienced and generates a helpful or affirming environment.

❖ Empathy is a highly effective communication ability that is underutilized by many. It permits one to comprehend the thoughts and resulting emotions of others. Also, it enables one to respond sympathetically to the feelings of others to gain their trust, which facilitates dialogue. Our fear of failure, rage, and irritation suddenly vanishes, allowing for a deeper conversation and more meaningful interactions.

❖ Empathy is more than just pity; it allows a person to comprehend others with compassion and understanding. Therefore, it plays a crucial role in a group project, where many individuals collaborate to accomplish something significant. It contributes to profound regard for friends establishing an atmosphere of harmony at school.

❖ Since empathy has far-reaching effects on our lives, you should at least try growing this ability so you can become better people, capable of sustaining friendships, and establishing stronger communities.

Over the past two decades, emotional intelligence has become a tool for developing the capacity to manage our and others' emotions. Empathy is one of the essential components of emotional intelligence skills.

How to Practice Empathy

The phrase empathy is typically, although not exclusively, applied to aesthetic experience. Perhaps the most obvious example is an actor or singer who sincerely feels his role. In other works of art, a viewer may feel engaged in what he watches or thinks through a form of introjection. The counseling style created by the American psychologist Carl Rogers relies heavily on empathy.

The practice of empathy may have its origins in the earliest days of human existence as neonates develop empathy by emulating their caregivers. There is no way to compare, measure, observe, prove or deny that the same feeling is experienced similarly by different people. Still, people can connect strongly, leading to greater understanding and emotional closeness.

Empathy is more crucial in social circumstances than it is psychologically. It indicates a healthy sense of self, self-awareness, self-worth, and in the positive sense, self-love. Without it, antisocial or psychopathic individuals can easily exploit and abuse others.

Since most social institutions that foster empathy, such as nuclear and extended family, clan, neighborhood, town, church, temple, or belief systems, have deteriorated in our time, narcissistic behavior has replaced empathy. This is largely represented in our popular culture's litigiousness, intolerance, and violence, as seen in the media, movies, video games, international relations, etc.

Empathy is the gateway to compassion, mercy, pity, altruism, and the joy of giving, contributing to a better and more civilized society.

Let's examine empathy in greater detail.

What purpose does empathy serve?

The objectives of empathy are:

❖ To demonstrate concern for another person.

❖ To cultivate meaningful, beneficial, and close relationships.

❖ To discover more about other individuals.

❖ To focus the conversation on significant emotional subjects.

❖ To reassure the other individual he is welcomed for who he is, encouraging him to open up.

❖ To lessen your annoyance with people by better understanding them. If you comprehend someone, you can forgive them.

❖ To eliminate bias and unfavorable presumptions, focus on the term "assumptions."

❖ To finally realize that everyone is understandable and that everyone's psyche can be porous.

Exercising empathy is challenging. Each individual acquires some empathy growing up and interacting with the environment, but how can we exercise empathy?

How to develop empathy:

1. Listen, listen, listen. The first step is to actively listen and respond. Listening is complex and everyone is susceptible to distractions. Even when we become sidetracked, we must refocus and get back on course to the best of our abilities.

2. One must cease comparing oneself to the other individual.

3. One must not recall their own experiences on the same topic while the other person is speaking.

4. The rhetorical back and forth cannot be viewed as an intellectual argument intended to demean the other party.

5. One must not believe he knows everything and hence does not need to listen to the other individual.

6. One must not disregard what the other person is saying or attempt to change the subject before it becomes severe.

7. One must stop assuaging the other person's feelings by agreeing with them. "I concur." "He did you wrong!" "What a jerk!" etc.

8. One must quit attempting to read the other person's thoughts.

9. One must cease considering his following action or response before the other person finishes speaking.

10. One must avoid censoring what the other person says by focusing on hearing only select topics or noteworthy statements.

11. One must not assume that the other person's statement is insane, extreme, infantile, dull, or hostile.

Let the other person know he is being heard. Nobody is perfect at this, but we can improve over time with practice. One way to accomplish this is to verbalize the other person's emotions. "This is quite painful to you." "You feel left out." "You feel unimportant." The emphasis on the other person's sentiments enables him to express and realistically investigate those feelings on his own.

It is unhelpful to ask too many questions, respond with judgment or offer premature advice or reassurance before the other person finishes speaking. It hinders the other person's ability to solve his situation on his own through communication. If you remember the other person's concern, suffering, or problem, telling him your own story or experience is not so horrible.

One of the most persistent causes of miscommunication is our emotional reaction to what the other person says. Suppose the speaker says anything that triggers an emotion (such as anger, insecurity, hurt, an insult to our beliefs, etc.) in the listener unrelated to the speaker. There, the listener may become distracted and misjudge the other person's situation.

A proper reaction captures the essence of the other person's emotions. This may sound like the listener is repeating the speaker, but it is an excellent approach to demonstrate attention and attentiveness, for example, "You feel offended" or "You are overwhelmed." If we do not react or comment while the other person is speaking, he may interpret our silence as disinterest or criticism or believe we do not understand him.

While the other person is speaking, an empathizer can predict what the other person is feeling and offer extra information. At such a time, at an appropriate point in the dialogue, nine interpretations of a question may improve the speaker's understanding of himself.

For instance, "Could it be that your mother is acting this way because she cannot bear the thought of losing you?"

Empathy is a valuable trait; nevertheless, reflection and empathy cannot create a flawless society on their own. Empathy generates feelings and acts that contribute to the improvement of societies. Because of this goal, empathy becomes the key that unlocks positive human contact.

CHAPTER 7
RESPECT

Children are like mirrors because they reflect much of what we say and do back to us. They acquire 95% of their knowledge through imitation, while only 5% is gained through direct instruction. They transmit what their parents teach, and they will speak the language they use.

Respect can infiltrate all spheres, including respect for oneself, loved ones, neighbors, and those with whom one disagrees philosophically. This is not simple to execute.

How can we approach this topic mindfully, so we don't lose sight of the significance of allowing others to have their feelings about things, as we want our thoughts to be respected?

As defined by the dictionary, respect is the "willingness to demonstrate deferential consideration, appreciation and have high esteem for another's viewpoint, wishes, and judgment." How can you hold someone in high esteem if you do not respect their principles and way of life?

To treat a person with the utmost respect is to recognize and uphold their inherent worth as humans.

❖   Are you upholding the ideals you regard to be most essential?

❖   Are you tolerant of yourself when you make mistakes?

❖   Are you willing to accept you've made a mistake when you're impatient and offend others with your words?

Even if most of us can handle the problems in our daily lives, there will always be times when everything feels out of control. The best action you can take is to review the situation. It is essential to remind yourself of the good things in your life. You must instill in yourself a sense of thankfulness.

Taking the time to respond to complex issues thoughtfully is an integral part of showing respect to others and yourself. Do you know how to respond politely when others ask you about shocking occurrences in the news or why individuals behave in ways at odds? Regardless of how strongly you feel about anything, it would help if you always answered with an open mind. You could respond, "I wonder what was going through that person's head when he did it."

You leave the option for discussion regarding how individuals make decisions. In this approach, you are respectful of yourself and your thoughts but also demonstrate to your friend that there are always multiple perspectives.

At this moment in history, respecting individuals of different nationalities and beliefs is one of the most challenging tasks. We may have different views, but we all have the same basic needs. We are similar because we all like to be warm, well-fed, and loved. What we believe beyond our physical bodies attempts to make sense of the universe.

Therefore, believe whatever brings you comfort and allow others to believe whatever brings them peace. This is a difficult undertaking for youth raised believing in a single religion. You need to be courteous toward others and recognize that they have been trained differently.

The best approach to learning respect is demonstrating respect for ourselves. When we experience respect, we understand what it feels like and how transformative it can be in our lives. Respect is a lifestyle value and respectful behavior helps you succeed in school and prepares the way for success in the workplace and marriage.

Consider these six suggestions:

1. Listen to others.

2. Listen deeply and intently.

3. Before responding, carefully consider what your friend wants and needs.

4. Remember that being honest will earn you the respect you deserve.

5. Always give the most truthful response possible. If this requires you to wait before responding, take your time.

6. Be willing to apologize if you talk angrily or too soon due to being busy or exhausted.

CHAPTER 8
KNOW YOUR WORTH

What's the first thing that comes to mind when you wake up in the morning? Is it how many followers I had overnight, What should I do next, where I need to go today, or what homework I need to finish?

How often do you consider your current state and what you require?

However, you forget that life exists for you, not vice versa. You will live your life from your inner core, not from your head or your thoughts, but you alone. The more regularly you check in with yourself, the easier life will feel since you will be more present in your own life.

It's comparable to reading a book while ignoring the outer world, this is the mind at work, composed of our thoughts and imagination. Try putting the book down for a while and simply being with only yourself. When we set aside our ideas, responsibilities, routines, and plans, we exist where we are, and we can see more clearly in this environment.

This does not exclude picking up the book again; nevertheless, it is sometimes beneficial to reset ourselves by deliberately attempting to be present inside ourselves and our environment. Remind yourself the next time you awaken to be, to wake up in the present rather than instantly engaging in your usual routine.

Take a minute during your day to be present now and be yourself. This includes clearing your mind, allowing your emotions to calm, trying not to do anything, and focusing on where you are and how you feel.

This is a grounding practice that helps you connect with yourself. It is acceptable to drift off, this is natural, but it takes only a second to regain focus if you try. It is satisfying even if you practice this very few times.

Being present with yourself is like giving yourself a break; it allows you to be with nothing, no wants, no actions, only yourself and where you are. This is fantastic. Allow your mind and emotions to relax and you can be present. You will then have a much greater understanding of yourself, your needs, and your life.

Create an Emotion Journal to use over the next one to two weeks. You will record your negative emotions in your journal each day as they occur. This will enable you to recognize your negative feelings and become aware of them as they arise throughout the day.

1. Recognize Your Negative Emotions

Every time you encounter a negative emotion (fear, anger, shame, guilt, or concern), write it down in your journal and elicit:

❖ What provoked or produced the feeling?

❖ How did I feel and what was the root of my emotions?

❖ In what context did I experience this emotion?

❖ Why did I feel the way I felt?

Ensure that you examine every scenario objectively. It is not about blaming others or yourself or being right or wrong; instead, it helps you understand your emotions and when and why they develop.

Be kind to yourself throughout this process. The objective is to stop yourself from responding to a circumstance with an undesirable or harmful emotion. The simple act of observing from the outside can allow you to modify your perception and establish a deeper connection with yourself.

2. Determine the Root Cause of Your Emotions

The next step is to determine the root cause. This phase is essential if you wish to comprehend why specific patterns or circumstances keep occurring in your life. Once you identify the underlying cause, you will better grasp your feelings and their significance.

This will allow you to recognize recurring patterns and make a deliberate decision about how you will behave next time. To determine the underlying cause, consider these queries:

❖ When did I first have this feeling?

❖ What incident may have caused these emotions?

❖ How did this experience make me feel?

3. Learn How Emotions Influence Your Life

The next stage is to identify and acknowledge this emotion's impact on your life by asking yourself these questions:

❖ What narrative am I telling myself about this circumstance?

❖ How has this narrative affected my life?

❖ What beliefs did I establish to validate or support my experience?

4. Let Go of Unwanted Feelings

Performing merely the first three stages will bring recognition to your life. Still, you want to go one step further and take the essential step of releasing your undesired feelings by asking yourself these questions.

❖ Am I ready to release this reactive emotion?

❖ Is this belief/story supporting me or undermining my happiness/success?

❖ Am I willing to abandon the narrative and form a new belief?

When a negative emotion arises, remind yourself that it is okay and instead of becoming annoyed or disturbed, say to yourself, "Here it is again: my old tale, my old belief, my old way of reacting." Take some deep breaths, release tension from your body, move your attention from your head to your heart and let go of the desire to think in favor of feeling.

Feel the sensations associated with the emotion. Observe it merely as a physical or biological sensation rather than a story you are attached to. It can also be beneficial to look down during this experience, as this helps you connect with your feelings, instead of looking up, which creates a mental state that generates thoughts that ultimately prevent you from connecting with your genuine emotions.

Now, you don't need to do anything, merely be with the experience. Observe what is occurring in the current moment, breathe and feel the emotion. Emotion is the mobility of energy. Determine the significance underneath your feeling. What is its motive?

Once you realize that emotion is simply energy traveling through your body, it will be much simpler to detach yourself from it. Feelings are not you and they only reveal your areas that require attention, comprehension, healing, and integration.

Resisting your emotions will produce an energetic magnet to more of the same unpleasant vibration, leaving you stuck and unable to move through them. You've heard the expression, "What you oppose persists."

Repressing your emotions will merely give the false sense that the issue has been resolved when you have prevented the full expression of how you feel, preventing it from dissolving on its own.

Emotional awareness will allow you to live life to the fullest and will benefit you in the long run. Check in with yourself every day and be aware of the messages your emotions are trying to convey to you. Accept them and move on. When dealing with your feelings, they are not your enemy.

5. Alter Your Unwanted Feelings

Please add a step to this exercise if, during this process, you realize that you most often retreat unconsciously to one significant recurring emotional state (for example, anger). If you have consistently defaulted to one emotion throughout your life, we cannot just remove that condition as doing so could leave you feeling empty or disoriented.

Once you have identified the primary unpleasant emotion you no longer wish to experience, choose a positive emotion to replace it in the future. Replacing an undesirable emotion with a desired (supportive) emotion will elevate you to a new energetic level where you can have a more meaningful life experience.

This step will propel you into a level of empowerment in which you are no longer a victim of your external world but a conscious co-creator of your existence.

Gain Confidence, Know Your Worth

Most of our decisions demand confidence and bravery and it takes a lot of guts to let someone know how you feel, particularly if that person has authority over you. To try new things requires confidence and the ability to prioritize oneself.

Fortunately, most of you can work on bolstering your confidence and courage. *Here are a few suggestions for how to accomplish it.*

1. *Recognize your confidence and courage.* Confidence is that "I can do it" sensation. Chances are you've felt it at some point. Perhaps it was before a game or immediately before a test for which you had diligently prepared. Contrarily, courage is not necessarily the absence of fear. Sometimes, courage is about being terrified and moving on with things anyhow.

2. *Start small.* To increase your self-assurance and bravery, take calculated risks where you have a strong possibility of succeeding. You could do this, for example, if you already know you can complete two of the three essential steps.

By achieving this first, you can acquire additional talents to pursue a more difficult objective, such as becoming a reading tutor. After gaining confidence by overcoming modest risks, you will feel prepared to take more significant chances. Each new obstacle might increase your self-assurance.

3. *Face your fears.* Dread can be your gut's way of alerting you, but excessive fear might prevent you from taking risks or pursuing your dreams.

Are you terrified of failing?

Are you terrified of appearing foolish? To overcome such worries, consider their origins.

Often, fear stems from discomfort with the unknown or a sense of helplessness. Occasionally, however, it is because you do not believe you deserve success. Please give yourself a lift by convincing yourself that you can accomplish it and are worth it.

4. *Do not stress over being flawed.* Many young women are on a "be-perfect treadmill." They believe they must appear and act flawlessly to be accepted and loved, but this is not the case.

You don't need to be number one all the time or do everything right. To gain confidence, avoid striving for perfection and live a little on the edge. Practice taking chances in situations where mistakes are inevitable.

5. *Find heroines.* The presence of heroines greatly assists in strengthening one's confidence and courage. Your hero or role model could be a member of your family, community, or the public, or she could be a person from the past. Determine which of your heroine's qualities and ideals you wish to possess and work to cultivate them in yourself.

Never is developing courage and self-confidence simple. However, we must develop both to act self-assuredly and to make the changes that will enable us to succeed in life.

CHAPTER 9
THE MEANING OF FRIENDSHIP

L ife is full of many individuals and identifying true friends may not always be simple. Therefore, it is advisable to be aware of the steps you can take to identify beneficial companions. First, we must determine who true friends are.

They are genuine individuals that care about everything you do. They don't come with pretense but are genuinely interested in your life. You may have had different acquaintances in your lifetime, and none of us has escaped the sorrow of nasty people. However, it is prudent to judge others fairly.

If you are cruel, you get what you get, the proverb goes. This is to suggest that if you were not a lovely friend, not surprisingly, you ended up with folks just like you. Since we all have defects, nobody can be flawless.

However, we are blessed with reasonable minds to recognize those who are good for us and those who are not. These pointers will help you distinguish those friendly buddies from those you should not waste time with.

Real friends are individuals who are kind and loving. Kindness and love are qualities best displayed via action and people cannot claim to be loving or kind without demonstrating it through their actions. Therefore, keep your eyes and ears alert regarding your pals.

Their actions will betray them. There is no way you could be fully duped. However, some friends pretend to be kind, so it is advisable to take your time. Because they cannot maintain a facade for an extended period, their true colors will eventually out.

Observe to determine if you have true buddies. Their attitude will assist you in recognizing friends. It is relatively simple to decide how people view things based on what they say.

You desire friends with an optimistic outlook or attitude toward life. Negative individuals are infectious, as are positive individuals. Nobody likes to be around individuals who are perpetually depressed about life.

To recognize true friends, you will receive assistance in times of need. Good friends will want to know about the difficulties in your life. When you are ill, they will be the first to soothe you and promise you everything will be okay. Real friends will be as concerned as family members since your relationship is so profound. This is visible in day-to-day life: many friends will stick tighter than a brother.

When you care for one another and do nice deeds, you will learn that friendships are unbreakable. Therefore, use the tips above to identify the types of people you should keep close. You will meet pals worth cherishing if you search diligently and have a positive outlook.

There are connections everywhere, including cell phones, the internet, Instagram, Twitter, Facebook, Tik Tok, and texting. You name it; we have a connection, but what about more than a cyber-connection or a faceless internet hyperlink?

Friendships are difficult to find in today's multitasking, fast-paced society. How should one seek friendship, and more importantly, how should one maintain a connection after it has begun?

Being yourself is among the most important things to remember while creating real friends. An authentic individual can maintain any relationship, whether platonic, professional, or romantic. People who pretend to be someone they are not will eventually reveal their true selves, at which point you will likely lose interest in them. You must also be able to discern the authenticity of others.

It will help if you discern which individuals are compatible with your true self. I'm not referring to the "friends" we met in summer camps semesters for weeks and then nothing; these are mere "context pals."

They only exist in the context provided. Work, neighborhood, and interest buddies are also included. The only way to find true friends with whom you can share most, if not all, of your life is to be true to yourself.

Another key to attracting genuine friends is remembering they are also seeking something. Give them something they can enjoy. If you go home, surf the net, and watch television, they have little to admire about you.

Try enrolling in a class, joining a gym, reading a book, or joining a group. People appreciate other individuals who are dynamic and intriguing. Remember to only participate in activities you genuinely enjoy. Do not participate in activities or events because you believe you will make friends there.

The secret to gaining good, genuine friends is to be the type of person that others desire as a good, genuine friend. When you do so, an unbreakable bond will be established, and a friendship founded on truthfulness will last.

How to Be a Helpful Friend

The true strength of a friendship cannot be determined until it is put to the test. The classic test of friendship is the requirement for assistance. When a person requires assistance from another, their relationship will either strengthen or weaken depending on the latter's response.

Considering this, it is essential to be a good friend in times of need to strengthen your ties. This is easier said than done since many individuals do not understand how to be friends in difficult situations. Here are my recommendations to assist you with this.

Listen First, then Offer Advice.

When a person has a problem or struggles with anything, they will likely confide in you and discuss their situation if they view you as a friend.

Many individuals erroneously believe that when this occurs, they should act as the expert and provide the other person with advice to assist them in solving their situation. However, you are not an expert, and the other person does not want you to tell them what to do.

First, your friend desires your consideration and focus. They expect you to listen to them with empathy. Simply talking about their problems and having someone listen to them will help them feel better and consider new solutions.

After attentively listening, you may next offer a few suggestions for handling the matter. You do not wish to play the expert; however, you want to share some of your views or experiences and describe what you might do in their circumstance.

Ask How You Can Assist and Assist

Besides listening, a good friend provides substantial assistance when the other person is in need. After understanding the other person's difficulty comprehensively through listening, ask how you may assist. You are doing this so it is evident that you do want to help them and so you can identify specific strategies to do so.

The greatest difficulty in genuinely assisting another person is that it costs time, effort, and occasionally additional resources. Therefore, when you aid a buddy, you use these resources when you could use them for yourself.

Whether you are helping a buddy finish a painting, go shopping or resolve a quarrel, or help study for a test, you are using your resources to benefit another person. You must recognize the importance of your connection and view this as a long-term investment.

If your friendship has value, supporting the other person is a means to strengthen it, and it will also give you benefits. It's a win-win situation, which is why assisting a buddy in need makes sense.

On the other side, you must recognize friendships that are not worth your time and effort. Some people are like sponges who constantly ask for favors but never return the favor. Such a friendship is like a one-way street; traveling down it is rarely worthwhile.

Developing connections that are mutually helpful and enjoyable is the key to a prosperous and fulfilling social life in the long run.

Accepting Differences

The absence of approval does not imply that a person would be compelled to conduct heinous atrocities. However, understanding the significance of acceptance is crucial when managing and leading others. Acceptance is one of the most successful tools for bringing out the best in people. However, it is challenging to demonstrate tolerance in the face of difference.

Regardless of how accepting we imagine ourselves to be, we are most comfortable with and so most accepting of those who are most like us. It is inherently human, and we must try much harder to postpone judgment and establish common ground with individuals on opposite sides of the spectrum.

Observing individuals who operate across functions is most exciting. Consider the technical and scientific individual who conducts controlled research studies to collect data.

They exercise caution when employing these data and figures by assuring their integrity and precision. Imagine this person talking with a salesperson who is more inclined to offer hypotheticals and estimates like, "What if we did it this way?"

In this circumstance, both parties possess unique talents, yet when confronted, they often fail to recognize their complementary brilliance and instead perceive barriers. They sense inaccuracy and insufficiency in one another.

They do not accept one another. Both parties fail to recognize the brilliance of the other, leaving them feeling irritated and unappreciated.

These events can also occur at home. For example, I recognize how challenging it is to welcome my sibling despite our differences continually.

- ❖ I am extroverted. She is reticent.

- ❖ I am outspoken. She is silent.

- ❖ I adore clothing and fashion. She does not care what she wears.

The list continues, and she's only eight!

My understanding of acceptance has taught me that agreeing is unnecessary. When you accept another person's differences, you abandon trying to change them. You might disagree with their method, but you accept it.

Here are important considerations to remember when you're confronted with a person who is so different from you you wish they could see things your way:

- Before focusing on their flaws, identify their positives. Often, their strengths will lie in areas where you are deficient.

- When communicating with them, seek to capitalize on their abilities.

- Recognize their shortcomings. No one consists solely of their strengths.

- Utilize your strengths when interacting with them, but do not persuade or convert them to your way of thinking.

It is not our purpose to make people feel unwelcome. Usually, we have urgent aims or ambitions, such as completing a project by its deadline, but discrepancies threaten that. Time, hurry, fear, and our limits often make it challenging to embrace the uniqueness of others.

In our increasingly complex society, the demand for acceptance is enormous. Whether you are an introvert or extrovert, I hope you are motivated to accept differences wherever that may be.

CHAPTER 10
FRIENDSHIP MANAGEMENT

After concluding that what we did was incorrect, we have many options. Will we consider the other person's losses? However, a morally just and spiritually sound person will view making amends as their only option.

Make Amends

Before approaching the other person, we must consider amends and establish a plan for what we must do and what we may be forced to do. However, adjustments are best made by consensus. If they are satisfied and we are vigilant enough to check, the outcome will likely succeed.

If the one who committed the wrong cannot recognize it, the process of making apologies cannot begin, and if both parties are in the wrong, it will almost take one to initiate the action!

What Form Must Amendments Take?

The amends must come with a spirit of service above and beyond the physical "form" of the amends. Amends work best when we are sincere and our integrity cannot be questioned—to the degree that we will be wrong, serve, and be obedient.

We cannot simultaneously make atonement and take the moral high ground. If we are to be sincere and genuinely observe the effectiveness of the amends, we must submit a submission considerate of their needs and shows patience.

Effects of Amends on Friendship

As if by magic, my troubled thinking is instantly alleviated because I am the controller of my fate; I can make reparations! In addition, I receive an empathetic retrospect instead. I immediately put myself in the other person's shoes. "Hmm ... this feels unusual." And this is all excellent!

Our relationships are typically jeopardized by the ever-widening abyss of conflict that results when neither partner recognizes their fault. These disputes prevent us from achieving peace; ironically, this is our golden key to revitalize your life.

The dis-ease we experience is beneficial since it is supposed to raise our awareness to make amends. If we have a functional friendship, we are prone to say and do harmful things to one another.

When we take a moral inventory and prepare to make apologies, we are well on our way to being healed from the inside out, regardless of the other person's response to our ultimate restitution.

Their reaction is mainly irrelevant as we have determined our guilt and responsibility and can rest assured that we are at least being honest and fair. The instantaneous adjustment in our approach to them augments the immediate drop in the terror we would have otherwise experienced. Even the fear can be eliminated, lifted from the circumstance. The objective is to gradually improve our relationship with them now that our hostility is gone. Things can only improve.

Set Expectations

We live in a society that expects us to discover our soul mate, settle down and sail through life without a hitch; you cannot expect much assistance from the people in your life.

There are benefits to having a goal. First, it provides a sense of direction. Second, it gives a sense of accomplishment. Its third objective is to provide a sense of security. The fourth is that goals are a measuring stick for what you wish to accomplish. To succeed in life in general, you must have a plan.

It would be best if you discussed the goals of the friendship. However, remember there should be no pressure on either of you; otherwise, your goal setting will become mandatory, which often suffocates the friendship and leads to its dissolution.

Also, lowering your expectations of each other will help preserve your connection. However, there is no universal remedy. This may be effective for some but not others. Who cares? If you want it to last, all possibilities should be examined, right?

The Value of Reasonable Expectations

Fundamental instincts are innate in all humans. Among these are the desires for safety, security, love, and companionship. Occasionally, however, if we allow it, our minds might run amok while meeting these impulses!

If you enable your imagination to run amok and focus on what you think to be your ideal friend, you may fall short of achieving your simple objectives. Excessive expectations can destroy a friendship before it even begins, leading to an endless cycle of searching for a nonexistent idealized individual.

Reality exists in the present, whereas imagination is what we wish existed. Often, these two things are opposites. What our vision feeds our senses can intoxicate them and the blind logic of desire can lead us into darkness. We could lose our ability to be objective.

The desire to experience can result in the conception of a fairytale hero or heroine based on unrealistic expectations. Such a storybook romance may appear innocuous on the surface, but attempting to turn such fantasies into reality can result in psychological destruction that may arise.

Living in a fantasy world might distort the good realities of a friendship and prevent it from ever succeeding.

CHAPTER 11
HANDLE CONFRONTATION

Managing conflict rarely appears in the job description of leaders or executives. But it appears on the to-do list of all leaders. Conflict and confrontation are inevitable throughout one's life.

Occasionally, confrontation happens with no warning. Other times, we are aware of its necessity and do our best in the heat of the moment. Although distasteful, we get through it.

There is a superior method. In all circumstances, we may prepare to handle conflict whenever and wherever it arises. This does not imply that the actual occurrence will be simple, and it does not always mean that things will unfold as we anticipate, but we will be better prepared to handle the problem. *Here are a few tips:*

❖ Before a confrontation, please develop your strategy for dealing with it.

❖ Record your thoughts on paper. Before a meeting, it is often preferable to resolve conflicts on paper.

❖ Know your emotional triggers and have coping mechanisms, so you don't "blow up" or "break down" when speaking with this person. Like an actor, visit those mental locations that will help you "feel" the confrontation. Note what triggers your anger. If you can identify it, you can take action and be better prepared for the event.

❖ Determine to be sympathetic. You are conversing with a person of respect and worth. Intentionally avoid saying or doing anything that violates your standards or demeans the other individual.

❖ Respect the individual and address their actions. Consider it now if you're looking for something extraordinary and sincere to acknowledge.

How can you offer significant facts while yet being respectful?

Separate facts from assumptions. Most individuals live their entire lives based on preconceptions, it's easy for the leader to have them. List your assumptions. The first point is the truth.

Anticipate potential answers and your responses. Almost invariably, a reaction will occur while confronting an opponent. How will you respond to stony silence, an onslaught of justifications, adamant denial, growing fury, or a breakdown into tears?

What occurs if they quit, agree with you, or request immediate assistance?

Having a plan and considering these possibilities beforehand will provide you with a helpful resource when needed. Practice potential discussions.

Role-play with another person:

If you are interested in refining your answers to confrontation, perform different role plays. Using your own words and approach when responding aloud will boost your confidence and help you refine your delivery.

Plan to be precise when outlining subsequent actions: If they are expected to act, be explicit about the nature of that action and the dates involved. Prepare to provide them with resources that will be beneficial. Provide positive alternatives for them to consider. If an appeal is possible, include contact information and details on the procedure.

In this most sensitive and potentially explosive of human interactions, be prepared. Take charge of yourself and the circumstance. Your preparation will bring you closer to reaching the required results while maintaining your integrity and expertise.

Conflicts have become an integral part of our daily lives; thus, knowing how to deal with them like an adult is necessary. In this section, I will attempt to demystify the appropriate execution of this process.

It is quite possible to attain peace of mind. However, I cannot guarantee it will be simple. When emotions run high, things spiral out of control, but if you are ready to exert effort and apply yourself, you can accomplish everything you set your mind to. I have learned on many occasions that the past significantly influences how you will respond to pressure.

If you have been seriously burned, the mere notion of it happening again will make you run for the hills. You can avoid it for some time, but you are delaying the inevitable, and you must ultimately face the consequences.

Ways to Deal with Disputes Maturely

The first step is Just Breathe; to calm yourself, you must learn the art of thinking before acting. You must think that this practice appears too basic to make a significant difference. My recommendation is not to criticize an idea you have not yet tried.

If it is so straightforward that you should have no trouble devoting a few minutes daily to it. Seek a peaceful location and take long, deep breaths.

Remove all negative thoughts from your mind as they only sap your energy. This is a complex technique to master since you will be continuously tempted to think about what you need to do. To prevent these situations, remind yourself that it will only take five minutes of your time.

Find a safe spot and count to ten as soon as you become irritated or someone provokes your anger. This is beneficial as it protects you from saying things in the heat of the moment you will regret later.

Second, take action; obviously, problems cannot be solved merely by contemplating them; there must be an accompanying action for things to occur. As soon as you have regained your composure, demonstrate that you have moved on from the conflict and are actively seeking solutions. Consider potential solutions if the problem keeps recurring.

Get some advice from your well-meaning buddies. If you need to confront someone about a particular issue, do it with a clear head. Prevent the situation from becoming violent.

When conversing with your friends, pay attention to the words you use. While describing your pain, try to grasp their perspective. Remember that if you show kindness, like sowing a seed, you'll enjoy the benefits of that compassion.

Another way to convince your loved one you are a great person despite the fight is to exhibit kindness. Focus on the positive aspects of a person. You will quickly understand that your condition is not as dire as you first believed and that others are enduring more challenging obstacles.

CHAPTER 12
RESIST PEER PRESSURE

Humans are social creatures who spend most of their lives interacting with others. Whenever people share anything in common, it is their nature to form tight bonds. Strong friendship relationships exist in all spheres of life where distinct groups of people join to socialize or join in activities.

This close interaction of humans brings with it these impacts on individuals. It would be tricky to remain in a group and simultaneously oppose their influence. People often follow their peer's code of dressing, language usage, facial and bodily gestures, and manner of reasoning. In reality, a person's behavior indicates the organization to which he belongs.

Influence can be beneficial or detrimental. Positive peer influence is the product of good company and is advantageous because it positively shapes one's character. When a vulgar and conceited individual desires to mingle with good and well-mannered people, he must alter his behavior to fit in with them.

But negative peer pressure occurs in poor company. It involves drug misuse, sex, crime, and rebellion. The only way to prevent it is to avoid association with inappropriate organizations. Otherwise, keeping one's moral convictions from being corrupted by one's morally corrupt companions would be difficult.

Besides retaining their ideals, one should never compromise them to gain the friendship of the wrong company.

Youth Peer Pressure and the Desire to Fit In

Peer pressure is not limited to a single age group; everyone needs to feel connected or at home within their age group. Peer pressure involves children and adults, and teens, like adults, are affected by their peer group because we feel the need to conform.

Peer pressure among adolescents is not merely a phase they pass through. Peer pressure is a potent reality, and many adults are unaware of its consequences, whether it leads to excessive hair styles and clothes, tattoos, or body piercing. It can harm the lives of children and adolescents, often leading them to experiment with tobacco, alcohol, and illegal drugs.

Teenagers prefer to associate with peers their age. Children, especially during puberty, spend a lot more time with their friends and less time with their families. This renders individuals more receptive to peer influence. It is essential to note that a youth's peers can positively influence them. Adolescents are more receptive to the sentiments and thoughts of their peers, and peers can and do serve as positive examples.

Select friends who share the same values and interests as you because they will probably not attempt to instill bad habits and behaviors in you. The right perspective includes achieving academic success, avoiding drug use, developing respect for others, refraining from smoking, and the avoidance of other dangerous behaviors.

Do you know why teenagers go wild sometimes? It's because young people engage in risky actions during adolescence as they attempt to discover their identity and become more independent. This makes them highly susceptible to experimenting with or becoming dependent on drugs and alcohol, sexual activity, and disobedience to authority, mainly if peer pressure is present.

Teens who use drugs are also more likely to be involved in gang activity, have low self-esteem, behavioral issues, poor academic performance, and depression.

Now let's address your parents, shall we?

While your parents, schools, religious and community leaders aim to create positive peer pressure among youth. Parents sometimes assume that teenagers do not appreciate their thoughts, whereas, in actuality, research indicates that parents have a significant impact on their children, particularly adolescents.

Here are suggestions for parents and other caregivers:

- Effective communication must always be maintained. Build a positive self-image.

- Keep your teen's activities under surveillance and role-play peer pressure situations to avoid scorn or shame.

- Don't hold back when discussing illicit activities like sex with others. Do not criticize the kid's friends as the teen may take this personally.

- Involve yourself in your children's lives.

- Listen attentively to what teenagers have to say and ask them questions.

- Youth groups and community events are great ways to get teenagers interested in the community and supervise their peers.

❖ Assist the adolescent in comprehending the difference between image (expressions of youth culture) and identity (who they are).

Peer pressure during adolescence and childhood enables the development of self-identity, healthy friendships, self-esteem, and self-reliance. Everyone should discuss their emotions, needs, and desires.

Parents wrongly believe that their adolescent does not wish to communicate with them. Yet, maybe the adolescent does not wish to discuss their poor grades, terrible behavior and how much difficulty they are in. Typically, adolescents are more inclined to discuss something that interests them or something nice about themselves.

Develop a daily habit of conversing with your teen. Developing a strong, close, and open relationship with your adolescent while he is young can make it simpler for him to communicate problems, concerns, and other sensitive matters related to school, relationships, and other sources of stress in his life.

Methods for Resisting Peer Pressure

I realize peer pressure sounds a bit high school and we encounter it predominantly during our high school years. However, it will still affect you in college, at work, and even online, and I am aware because I also feel it.

Always wanting to "belong" or blend in wherever we are causes us to feel stressed, and that's human instinct. However, mishandling it might occasionally put us at risk for undesirable effects.

With that being said, here are effective ways to resist peer pressure:

Learn to refuse

Yes. That is correct! Saying "no" to your pals does not make you less of a friend or an alien. If you know what your friends are doing will produce adverse outcomes, learn to disagree.

Let your voice out. You do not have to engage in the same activities as your buddies constantly. Instead, try to convince them otherwise. Always remember that a true friend would never intentionally harm another.

Know your limits

If your pals invite you to party one night, but you have class or work the following night, place a rain check on the invitation. You do not have to sacrifice your work or study for such things. If your friends consider you a "killjoy" let them be. However, remember that a good friend will always comprehend your predicament. Try to make amends with them at least once more.

Don't Live beyond Your Means

Today's technological breakthroughs make it simple to stalk other people. With just one click, we can readily know what they're buying, what they're wearing, or where they're going. Humans occasionally fall into the trap of desiring the same things. If a buddy or someone else has purchased the newest iPhone or latest Jordan, you do not have to do the same.

If you have the ability or the means to purchase it, go ahead. However, if your parent's finances are limited, you should reconsider. Going with the latest trend doesn't always make you "in." Ten years from now, none of those materialistic things will fit, they will be out of style, but being yourself and enjoying your current things is sufficient to set you apart.

Be authentic!

Being in a group means we copy what others do, even if it makes us uncomfortable. What is the reason? Because we want to be accepted, but to be accepted, never hide in the shadows of others. Be authentic. There is nothing more attractive than a genuine person.

Select the right companions

Have you ever heard the adage, "Show me your friends and I'll show you your future?" The greatest approach to fighting and avoiding peer pressure is carefully selecting the company you keep. Surround yourself with people who will inspire you to do great things, respect your limits, tolerate your flaws, and accept you regardless of who you are.

The individuals we choose to be with will either pull us down or lift us up. Being with the right person could well improve our quality of life.

Peer pressure occurs in many forms. It is up to us if we let it get into our system. We just must be strong and know our priority is for us not to be carried away by this pressure.

You all yield to peer pressure for different reasons. Most of you spend as much time with your peers as you do with your parents, siblings, or relatives. Some of your classmates might also be your closest pals, making it extra tough not to give in to their requests and ideas. Peers can become like family. Because you care about your peers as you would for your siblings and family, they might exert significant pressure on you to agree with their requests.

Peer pressure is therefore tough for even the most disciplined to resist. Even when you know something is wrong and dangerous, you may wind up going along with it if you aren't careful to say "no" and mean it.

Here are many instances in which you may succumb to peer pressure.

1. *You desire to be liked.* Most of you want to be appreciated by others and believe that by going along with your peers, they will like you more. This is not always the case, however.

2. *You want to appear cool,* but if you do something that terrifies or frightens you, you may be causing yourself harm and suppressing your values. This is not cool in any way.

3. *You do not wish to disappoint your peers.* Your classmates often have different views about what they want you to do with them daily. Therefore, if you assert yourself, you will not necessarily disappoint people, but you will demonstrate that you have differing opinions.

4. *You do not wish for anyone to be angry with you.* Sometimes, asserting yourself helps reduce the hostility of other children. If your peers genuinely care what you believe, they should not be offended when you disagree with them. Instead, they should respect your viewpoints even if they disagree.

5. *You don't want to be made fun of.* True friends and peers do not make fun of you if you do not follow their lead. They merely allow you to act as you deem appropriate.

6. *You don't want to be left out.* If your peers care about you, they will not make you feel excluded if you do not participate in a particular activity. They will allow you to decide for yourself what you will agree to and will not agree to.

7. *You are concerned about losing a friend.* True friends and peers do not harass you or threaten to end your friendship if you disagree with something they believe in. Instead, they are interested in your opinion on what they are about to accomplish.

Don't give in the next time your friends and peers ask you to do something uncomfortable; instead, establish yourself. Your peers may regard you more highly and you will undoubtedly respect yourself more.

CHAPTER 13

EMOTIONAL MANAGEMENT AND MEDITATION

Many teens get in trouble with the police only because they want to prove how "in command" they are of their lives. According to psychologists, these adolescents have varying emotional and behavioral issues and often take a defiant and antagonistic attitude. They will undertake outrageous things as if they are attempting to show off.

They do not realize at first that although they give the impression of being in charge, they are out of control of their lives as they are expelled from schools, community activities, and peer groups. They often think of society as their enemy and flirt with the thought they are outcasts, yet these are effects of their behavior, not the causes.

One day, a counselor asked one of these adolescents whether he wants to be an enslaved person or an enslaver if given the option. The adolescent promptly responded, "The master, of course."

The counselor replied, "Then why do you choose to be a slave?"

He intended to convey that he and other children who have fallen into similar deliquescent patterns have lost control of their life because they have become emotionally enslaved people. By not managing your emotions, you act rashly and foolishly, which could bring you into problems in some circumstances.

Teenagers often link themselves with rebels and do not like being enslaved or told what to do. The problem may be viewed from a different perspective if it is reframed.

Acting upon instinct proves that one is not a "master" of one's emotions and has little control over them. This implies "servitude." Many psychologists embrace this conception when dealing with adolescent criminality. The effort to convince people to modify their behaviors must begin with assessing their willingness and preparedness to alter. This process starts with the pre-contemplation stage, in which the individual says, "I'm fine the way I am." In this stage, interventions like inciting fear or imparting instruction induce short-term or no change in someone's behavior.

To drive change in the mentioned stage, it is recommended to reframe the problem in a way that combines self-interest and a chance for self-control. Therefore, the individual must be allowed to change her conduct only if she desires a better life.

For instance, a person visits the dentist and undergoes extensive dental work. The dentist suggests that she floss her teeth every night to heal completely. The patient responds that he is too busy. Instead of attempting to scare or educate the patient, the dentist responds, "Okay, just floss the teeth you wish to keep." In this approach, the patient is provided with the proper framework for problem management, which increases the possibility of success.

Establish Emotional Limits

Most adolescents struggle to define their emotional boundaries and many youngsters cannot even control their emotions. Even adults may have difficulty establishing their emotional boundaries. Therefore, teenagers must develop the practice of setting emotional boundaries as early as is feasible.

Emotional boundaries define your genuine sentiments and responses to particular people, objects, and situations. It will help if you always protect your borders. Boundaries indicate where your emotions finish, where another person's begin, and what you will and will not tolerate. Establishing and maintaining these boundaries will provide your heart and soul with the space to feel secure before speaking or acting.

Here are some strategies for establishing emotional boundaries.

- ❖ Always pay attention to your heart and what it is telling you. Maximum introspection is required to determine your genuine emotions. If something doesn't feel right, trust your intuition.

- ❖ Do not place too much faith in others. Before divulging personal information, we must take the time to get to know individuals. If we are not careful, we will be injured. Instead, get to know the other person before extending trust.

- ❖ Accept no psychological abuse from others. When someone is rude or aggressive to you for the first time, cut all ties with that individual; their behavior could have a dangerous effect on your sense of self-worth. If someone is consistently abusive, avoid them.

- ❖ Spend time with positive and supporting individuals. Negative individuals can make you feel horrible about yourself and hopeless. However, if you surround yourself with joyful individuals, you will feel inspired and confident, and who knows, perhaps you will also feel empowered. You need this mental stability to enter adulthood emotionally fit.

❖ Establishing emotional boundaries will protect your most sensitive sensations and emotions. Develop solid boundaries to prevent abuse from others and permit yourself to express your feelings freely. It takes time to establish these limits. Try not to rush it.

❖ If you can develop these behaviors as habits, all the better. You will be significantly more confident as a teenager, and you will continue to grow in confidence as a young adult.

Meditation

Did you know that teens can benefit significantly from meditation? As they grow older, they appreciate more the privilege of having some time to fully focus on the present and disengage from thoughts about everything else.

The first step in changing our thoughts and redirect where our life is heading is to be aware of those little quiet thoughts. With fifteen minutes of daily meditation for at least three weeks, the brain becomes more responsive and less reactive. The goal of meditation is not for you to stop thinking. Some thoughts will catch your attention while you're meditating, and others won't. When something does, acknowledge it and then redirect the focus back to your breathing. There are several types of meditation, but let's talk about the most used among teens.

Counting Meditation

Sit or lie on your back and count slowly in your mind from 100 to one; counting backward requires more concentration and will help you stay more focused. Try not to think about other things and stay with the numbers. If you lose your count, start again from 100. If you reach one, stay in silence for a few more moments.

This is a great exercise for developing concentration, and if you can focus enough to reach one without getting distracted, you will have a beautiful and very relaxing inward experience. Try it and see for yourself!

Breathing Meditation

Sit up straight and close your eyes. Breathe deeply enough that you can hear your breath. Feel how the breath moves your body and notice the flow of the breath through your nostrils, in and out of your body. Try to feel the contact of the air with the inside of your nose or how the air touches your upper lip. Now gradually make your breath much gentler and let it flow naturally but keep listening to its sound. Try not to listen to your thoughts; listen only to your breath. Whenever you think of other things, come back to your breath. You can practice the same meditation by listening to your heartbeat and bringing your full attention to it similarly.

Compassion Meditation

This meditation can be challenging at times, and I mention that forgiveness and sending love to people who have harmed us is more of a healing process for us than finding a reason or giving an excuse for the wrongs done.

Sit comfortably or lie on your back with your eyes closed. Breathe deeply and bring your attention to your heart, directing your breath. Now, inside your heart, see an image of yourself. See yourself happy and healthy; see yourself realizing all your dreams and having everything you ever wanted for yourself. Repeat, *"May I enjoy happiness."* Keep repeating this in your mind for about a minute.

That's all there is to it. Meditation makes you more aware of your thoughts. Therefore, those thoughts can be changed, improved, or eliminated. The thoughts you are not mindful of are the ones that make you feel what you feel and want what you want and push you into actions you might not have done with more conscious thought. On your free time, you might wat to explore other types of meditation, you might surprise yourself and even find yourself enlightened.

CHAPTER 14
LIFE CHALLENGES

Sexual Assault (Rape)

No one may touch your body without permission; if they do without your consent, then you have been assaulted. Like you don't have the right to hit, touch, or harm anyone else without their consent, no one has the right to make you feel uncomfortable.

Consent doesn't apply only to sexual situations. Consent is about respecting other people's boundaries. As a nurse, when I get a new admission from the emergency room, they must sign a consent to treat. I ask permission to touch them before doing a physical assessment, it's a sign of mutual respect, and they trust me not to violate that trust. Consent is required whenever you interact with someone else's body, property, or reputation. Want to borrow your friend's jacket? Ask for permission (consent) first. Get it?

Have you heard of teen rape? It is prevalent, especially "date rape." The issue is that most of these rapes go undetected, and you may wonder why many victims do not report the rape or the abuse. The most prevalent causes are anxiety and guilt. Fear of what other people will think. Fear of having a sexually transmitted disease or being pregnant. Fear of the consequences of "telling" or reporting the abuser to the authorities. Fear of having to confront the abuser(s) again.

Typically, the guilt stems from the individual's perception they bore some responsibility for what transpired. Were they dating their abuser, had dated them, knew the abuser, or were under the influence of drugs and alcohol at the time of the rape, their guilt may be intensified. Therefore, what will happen to these victims if they continue without reporting the rape or abuse?

They are statistically more likely to perform poorly in school. They frequently engage in hazardous, self-destructive activities, including drug and alcohol misuse and unprotected sex. The anger, embarrassment, and stress they experience can result in eating disorders, despair, and even suicide. If not treated, these habits can continue until adulthood.

Are You a Teen with a Fear of Disclosure?

If you are a teen victim of rape, sexual assault, or sexual abuse, please remember this. It makes no difference if you were drinking, taking drugs, dating the guy or lady, passed out, or anything else! If you said, "NO," or hinted "NO" or could not agree, it was teen rape, and YOU WERE NOT TO BLAME! You were taken advantage of! If you tell no one, that person will likely continue to harass others!

Many other teens have also experienced rape. I understand it isn't very comforting to tell someone, but you must do it yourself! The perpetrator of your rape or assault took something from you without your consent!

Alcohol or drugs are NOT an excuse. The essential question for you is whether you consented. Both partners must be conscious (awake and aware) and willing to engage in sexual activity. In addition, it is a crime if the individual who raped you was older than 18 years old. If you are feeling alone, confused, and terrified, that is typical given what you have been through. However, consuming alcohol, taking drugs, engaging in risky behaviors such as having unprotected sex with several people, and punishing yourself will NOT alleviate the agony you feel within! DO YOU HEAR ME?

The only way to feel better is to confide in a trusted someone. That is the first step in reclaiming your life! You are considerably stronger than you believe. Many adolescents have been in your position and have prevailed, as will you. TRUST ME ON THAT!!

Drug Abuse

Addiction to drugs affects everyone, especially adolescents. Drug abuse among adolescents has never been more prevalent than it is today. So, what constitutes teen drug abuse? Can any indicators indicate this behavior or habit? What are the impacts or repercussions?

Substance misuse among adolescents is widespread and continues to spread. This action's both short-term and long-term repercussions are highly harmful.

High mortality rates among individuals between the ages of 15 and 24 are mainly attributable to alcohol and drug misuse. Substance misuse can also lead to unwanted and violent behaviors, such as committing rape or murder, harassing, or attacking another person, or stealing or robbing.

Meanwhile, some adolescents may utilize substance abuse as a coping method for anxiety or sadness. They may view drug usage as an escape from the troubles and stresses of daily life. Behaviors such as running away from home, avoiding other family members, and associating with undesirable individuals can indicate drug use or abuse.

Teens with social skills and a family history of substance abuse are more likely to engage in destructive behavior. Teens can be influenced to try drugs and develop a drug-seeking attitude. They must be assisted by involving them in more useful pursuits, such as athletics. They should also be able to express their creativity through the arts. This should be done to divert adolescents away from drug misuse and its consequences.

Substance misuse among adolescents may have these effects:

❖ Extreme irritation

❖ Insomnia, sleep deprivation, or disturbed sleeping habits

❖ Convulsions

❖ Emotions of angst and melancholy

❖ Paranoia

❖ Memory loss and issues with cognitive function (slow learning)

❖ Daily coughing accompanied by phlegm

❖ Lethargy

❖ Teeth grinding or clenching

❖ Dehydration and even death from overdose

These effects of adolescent drug addiction can be averted or prevented from worsening. Change begins with the desire to do so; however, this is insufficient. You need to seek treatment. If you have a friend who has succumbed to teen drug misuse, get help, contact their parents and they will do whatever is necessary to get the help needed from a drug rehabilitation center or institution. They offer specialized adolescent drug treatment programs that can help a teen get back on track and recover.

Depression

Teenagers' desire to express their independence from parental and other authority is a normal aspect of maturation. A portion of their "rebelliousness" might be linked to the hormonal changes they are coping with. The teenage years are filled with uneasiness towards the opposite sex, conformity pressure, and low self-esteem, all of which can lead to depression.

Symptoms of Depression in Teenagers

Because adolescents are already dealing with many other challenges, others around them may confuse adolescents with depression with adolescents seeking their identities. While some severe actions may lead to depression in adolescents, some circumstances are considerably more likely to trigger an episode of sadness.

Some symptoms of depression include irritability; defiance; reckless behavior involving alcohol, drugs, and sex; a desire for solitude and indifference to social activities; a loss of interest in school accompanied by poor grades; and feelings of sadness and inadequacy can lead to suicidal ideation.

Reasons for Teenage Depression

If you know a teenager who has just suffered one of these incidents, you may assist him by keeping an eye out for any subsequent behavioral changes that indicates depression. Adolescents do not differ from anyone else when it comes to their reactions to the death of a loved one, difficult family life, or the termination of a relationship. Because of incidents of bullying or other forms of abuse, depression and adolescence often coexist.

Most adolescents still depend on their parents, family members, and friends for physical care and social reinforcement, despite their efforts to forge their identities. Deprivation of these might result in intense tension and overpowering feelings of uneasiness. This profound insecurity, along with the sensation of confusion brought on by the hormonal changes of adolescence, is one of the key causes of depression in adolescents.

Unless recognized and treated, adolescents with depression may engage in self-destructive behaviors such as cutting and sexual promiscuity. They may direct their rage within and contemplate other escape paths, if not discovered and treated, they may suffer for the rest of their life from the repercussions of their depression-controlled behaviors. Get Help!

Obesity

The prevalence of obesity among adolescents is a developing problem. Teenagers with weight problems must be treated before it is too late or they will have chronic mental and/or physical illnesses later in life. Teenage obesity should therefore be prevented while adolescents are still young.

A balanced diet containing various essential nutrients, including proteins, carbs, vitamins, minerals, fats, salt, and water, is the key to weight loss in adolescents. They require a diet rich in vitamins, carbs, minerals, fats, salt, and water to succeed. The second most significant factor the adolescent should consider is participating in numerous sports and other activities. While the adolescent is on a diet, it is a good idea for them to visit a physician for advice and motivation.

The adolescent should remember that losing weight is no simple task. The procedure will take months or even years, depending on their circumstances. For effective dieting, it is suggested that the adolescent prepare meals at home rather than purchasing them outside as this may result in improper nutrition.

Creating a realistic strategy for how much weight the adolescent wishes to lose is a realistic place to start; however, lowering calories rapidly is not the way to go. Proteins, nutrients, and carbohydrate levels should always be remembered to prevent a decline in nutritional status.

Teens who wish to reduce weight should engage in sports and other physical activities, but walking is an excellent option if they are not accustomed to being active. Whether you walk your dog, your neighbor's dog, or with friends, it is necessary to get the body moving.

If you dislike walking, cycling is an excellent exercise method. If the teenager cannot ride a bicycle, jogging might provide an amazing workout. Sports such as basketball, tennis, swimming, etc., are both enjoyable and effective for fat loss. A teenager should consume an average of two liters of pure water daily to stimulate their metabolism and flush their body of toxins and wastes. Remember to obtain adequate sleep, perhaps eight hours will be enough. The benefits of sleep are sometimes undervalued, although the management of carbs, proteins, and other nutrients is a crucial benefit too.

Self-Harm

Self-harm is any deliberate attempt or acts to injure oneself. So, the term is straightforward, but self-harm includes non-suicidal self-injury, any self-harm inflicted without intent to die, and suicide attempts. Suicide attempts are a form of self-harm and the difference between the two lies in whether the person inflicting injury on himself means to die by doing it.

Making cuts and scratches on oneself is the most common self-harm. Some teens do other forms, such as burning themselves deliberately or hitting themselves, striking themselves with a fist, or headbanging.

If you feel that way, it's usually a proverbial cry for help, trying to express some emotion or demonstrate distress too difficult for you to articulate in words. You may not be ready to talk about what's hurting you but believe me when I say it's never okay to take a life or to cause harm for whatever reason you might think of. Therefore, it's important to learn to deal with the emotions surfacing even when they're too hard to acknowledge. It's important to talk to your parents about those feelings so they can better help you. We mentioned meditation before and learning to control your thoughts, and another way to do that during the day is through positive affirmations.

Affirmations are positive, caring messages for us to give ourselves; they can be good things to say to ourselves to help us feel better. You can also write them up on the wall in your room, in your bathroom mirror, or even on your fridge to look at during hard times. It sounds quite crazy, but it works! Self-care affirmations can help boost your mood and attitude, leading to a positive day ahead in achieving your well-being goals.

Acknowledge that your feelings are real and vital, and you will talk about them instead of acting on them. There are good reasons for the pain you feel, but it doesn't have to last forever. You deserve the support you need to get over the things that hurt you. You are a real, worthwhile, good person and deserve to live the life you were meant to. You don't deserve to hurt yourself or anyone else. You are LOVED ☺

Below is a list of affirmations, there are no right way or wrong way to go about them, but when you repeat them, believe what you say:

1. *"I always know exactly what to say and do."*

2. *"My self-care is my priority, no matter how sad I am today."*

3. *"Today, I will be kinder to myself than yesterday!"*

4. *"It's okay if things don't go as planned because it doesn't mean that the whole day has been ruined."*

5. *"The only person who can change me is ME—nobody else but MYSELF."*

6. *"All of my dreams are possible through self-discipline and belief in myself."*

7. *"Every single thing happens for a reason, even when we cannot see why at first."*

8. *"Everything I need comes from within me; therefore, there is no need to look for it elsewhere."*

9. *"I will not let the negativity in others affect me today."*

10. *"Today, I choose self-love instead of self-hate."*

11. *"Negativity is always self-destructive, so I won't choose it!"*

12. *"I am self-aware; therefore, I can learn from my mistakes."*

13. *"You are never too old to become who you want to be!"*

14. *"My life is rewarding and fulfilling because of the choices I make each day."*

Stress

The reality regarding adolescents and stress is that physiological stress exists for adolescents and adults. With all the pressures in the modern world, it is unnecessary to be a disturbed teen to experience stress. It bothers me tremendously so many of these young lives are influenced by something they do not fully comprehend.

Stress is the brain's natural reaction or response to a perceived or actual threat to the body. The stress response occurs automatically. The brain aids in our survival automatically. It is similar to how the brain automatically instructs the body to breathe throughout the day. The stress reaction notifies us when our natural equilibrium is disturbed, whether the threat is genuine or perceived, and the stress reaction reacts or responds to all these aspects of everyone, including adolescents.

With teenagers and stress, it is essential to recognize that most of their stress stems from the daily uncertainty they confront. Cognitive stress or feelings of uncertainty bring on the continual activation of the stress response. Why? For example, when one teenager makes fun of another, the brain often responds as it would if that person had hit you in the nose. These words would be regarded as a threat to your survival by the brain. Because of feeling threatened, the stress reaction is activated, and we fight or flee. Remember that the brain's purpose is to ensure our survival. Therefore, a teen's perception of a frightening scenario will be regarded as requiring a protective response.

Ask yourself the following thoughts of uncertainty and anxiety, even if you are a troubled or stressed-out adolescent.

* Does your family's financial situation impact you?

* Have your parents ever been divorced?

* Has someone you loved died?

* Are you overwhelmed by the obligations of school?

* Do you believe there are many expectations of you?

* Do you believe you do not belong socially?

* Do you feel unsafe?

* Do you struggle to manage your hectic schedule?

* Are you battling to keep your grades up?

* Do you or does a person you know suffer from substance abuse?

If you replied "yes" to any of the questions listed above and have been dealing with stress for an extended period, you may need assistance coping with stress.

So, what are the emotional effects of stress on adolescents? Contrary to what many believe about emotions, they are not spontaneously generated. Thinking always precedes an emotional response, whether positive or negative, happy or sad, and there is always an originating notion.

Emotional stress can be overwhelming for adolescents, manifesting in teen depression, teen substance misuse, stress and anxiety, out-of-control adolescents, and adolescents with low self-esteem. I believe in the curative power of equilibrium and the results from more frequent use of the relaxation response. The most encouraging message I wish to impart to teenagers regarding stress is that much of what you struggle with is likely due to mismanaged stress. In combating stress, the only requirement is a willingness to study stress-reduction techniques like meditation and affirmations.

CHAPTER 15
INTERNET SAFETY

What Is Cyberbullying?

Social media networking has enabled people from different parts of the world to connect, learn more about themselves, and forge lifelong friendships. Even long-lost acquaintances and family members have been reunited thanks to these services and platforms. However, the new technology has also brought a curse along with its benefits. This curse is cyberbullying. Internet bullying happens when adolescents use the Internet, cell phones, or other electronic devices to transmit or upload text or images intended to injure or humiliate another individual. Cyberbullying is on the rise alongside the rising usage of technology.

Cyberbullying is prevalent due to the bully's ability to operate anonymously and cast a wider net. He not only bullies you, but he also draws in further bullies. Because he hides behind a computer screen and is supported by other bullies, he feels even more emboldened to torture his victim. It may be a surprise that girls are the most prevalent violators by the time they reach middle school.

Cyberbullying is considerably more extensive than harassment on the playground or in the school cafeteria. It occurs on the Internet, utilizing social networking sites such as Facebook, Instagram, TikTok, or chat rooms affiliated with gaming websites. Bullies also use text messaging to send messages to their whole contact list. With all the fast global communication tools available today, you can imagine that a bully's sphere of influence extends well beyond the playground.

Computers, tablets, laptops, and smartphones have become part of our daily lives with the advent of technology. Today, virtually no one can survive without these devices. Over the past few decades, the communication industry has undergone a revolution that has effectively shrunk the globe. People in different corners of the world may now instantly speak with one another because of the Internet.

Cyberstalking is an additional type of cyberbullying. It may involve false accusations, uncomfortable observations, threats, identity theft, the destruction of data or equipment, the recruitment of children for sexual activity, or collecting information for harassment. Women are the most common targets of cyberstalking. Even when there is no physical or vocal contact with the stalker, it can be just as scary and frightening as other types of crime. This crime can cause victims to exhibit significant psychological and emotional reactions. Changes in sleep habits, despair, anxiety, wrath, paranoia, shock, and disbelief may ensue.

The Danger

This issue has become a growing threat, especially among adolescents. Using text messages or email rumors delivered by email or uploaded on social networking sites and embarrassing photographs, videos, websites, or bogus accounts constitute cyberbullying.

Cyberbullied individuals are sometimes victimized in person. In addition, while the source of cyberbullying is often unknown and cannot be prevented, it's challenging to avoid it. It can occur seven days a week, 24 hours a day, even when a person is alone. Offensive remarks and images can be submitted anonymously and quickly spread to a vast audience and tracing their origin can be difficult and even impossible. After receiving or posting, it is complicated to delete inappropriate or annoying messages, texts, and images.

The Emotional Effect

Although social networking platforms do not promote such heinous acts, they are a vehicle to carry them out. Children and women are the most common targets of cyberbullying, which can significantly affect the mind. Victims of this heinous crime may endure behavioral changes such as rapid and extensive use of alcohol and drugs, an inclination to skip school, bullying in person, unwillingness to attend school, poor grades, decreased self-esteem, and irregular health problems.

Suggestions for Preventing Cyberbullying

If you are a victim of either of these two forms of bullying (or any other type of bullying), you should not keep it to yourself. This issue can be resolved with the assistance of parents, family members, close friends, or professional counselors. The incident should be reported to the police so the perpetrator can be identified and apprehended as soon as possible.

As cyberbullying increases, it is essential to understand how to prevent it. *Here are our top ten preventative measures against cyberbullying.*

1. Educate Yourself

Few adolescents will sit at a computer and research internet bullying. Let you be the exception, stop and report cyberbullying and reassure others that disclosing bullying incidents to a responsible adult is safe. The first step in combating cyberbullying is a thorough understanding of it and where it might occur.

2. Safeguard Your Password

Don't share your password with anybody, not even close friends. Protect your password and other sensitive data from prying eyes. Also, never leave passwords where others can find or view them.

3. Keep images "family friendly"

Think twice before posting that photo of you partying with friends or posing seductively. Only submit photographs you want your parents, grandparents, and the world to see. Bullies can use inappropriate images to harass you and make your life difficult.

4. Only Open Messages from People You Know

Never open an email, Facebook message, or other messages from an unknown sender. These messages may contain malware that can infect your system and many of these infections will collect your data.

5. Don't Forget to Log Out

Keeping passwords on your computer or phone may make your life easier, but you must also take care not to expose yourself. If you lose your cell phone or allow someone to use your computer, they can access all your information and assume your identity online.

6. A Transfer Can Affect Your Future

With today's technology, we are urged to post anything that comes to mind. However, doing so could damage your reputation. You may not understand how many people will see and judge you based on what you publish. Human resource departments and school administrations now research an applicant's online presence before accepting or hiring them, which is why it's essential to exercise caution before posting.

7. Raise Public Awareness of Cyberbullying

Many individuals lack a comprehensive understanding of what cyberbullying is and what it entails. You can organize a program, campaign, or event to raise awareness about cyberbullying. Educating others is an important step in combating cyberbullying.

8. *Examine Privacy*

Virtually all social networking sites allow users to restrict access to their online profiles to only those they know. In protecting yourself, it is crucial not to grant access to unknown individuals.

9. *Verify Your Online Reputation*

Regularly "googling" yourself is one strategy to defend yourself against unwanted bullying and harassment. Enter your name into any major search engine to ensure no private information or images appear. If you discover something you want to be erased, take immediate action.

10. *Treat Others as You Would Wish to Be Treated Yourself*

Do not engage in cyberbullying yourself. Respect and treat people as you would like to be treated. Do not harass or say harsh things to others online.

CHAPTER 16
REACH OUT FOR HELP

We are not naturally inclined to seek help. We often find it excruciatingly difficult to do because it makes us feel vulnerable, weak, or ashamed; therefore, our concerns about rejection and embarrassment prevent us from acting.

In actuality, the only true weakness is refusing help. The most intelligent people I know recognize that they do not know everything and seek others to fill in their knowledge or skill gaps.

Life is about learning and growing; we all require help during difficult stretches. Beyond every difficulty is an opportunity for progress, and by asking for help when we're in need, we uncover solutions, get fresh perspectives, and ultimately become more capable.

Why It Is Wise to Request Help

If you ask for help, you will discover that it arrives and your needs are met, often exceeding your expectations! *Consider these reasons why it is wise to ask for help when stuck:*

❖ If you ask for help, you will probably receive it! Why not take constructive action instead of attempting to address your problems by keeping them concealed?

❖ Asking for help allows you to manage your energy better. Life balance is all about energy management. When you ask for help with a challenge, you have more energy for other pursuits.

❖ It creates fresh opportunities to engage with people. Requesting help makes people aware of how they can assist us and improves interpersonal bonds.

❖ By requesting help, we open the door to learning. By being receptive to the input of others, we improve our growth and consciousness.

❖ We recover our power by overcoming fear and accepting the challenge of asking! Our greatest gifts lie beyond the things we fear the most; thus, ask for help even when you fear the consequences and you will reclaim your power!

How to Request Help

Knowing how to ask for help is also crucial to seeking help. *Here are a few suggestions to remember the next time you need help:*

❖ Request help as soon as you discover you require it. Problems that go unresolved often amplify and become enormous issues that sap energy and resources.

❖ Recognize that everyone (including you!) deserves help as through mutual support we all grow and prosper.

❖ Recognize that the only thing you have to lose is your fear. If the person you approach can assist you, you will gain knowledge from the encounter. If they reject you, you can approach someone else.

❖ Consult someone you can trust. If they do not know the solution themselves, they probably know someone who does.

❖ Be specific about your needs. The best words to use are "I require your help." Straightforward and to the point!

❖ Provide as many specifics as possible. Even if you don't know the issue, describe what you know about the situation and what you require.

❖ Acquire a commitment. Inquire if they can assist you and in what capacity. A commitment will put your mind at ease and eliminate anxiety. Even if they cannot assist you, they may offer helpful advice or recommend someone who can. In any case, you will benefit!

❖ Record the solution to your difficulty for future reference after discovering it. You may reencounter the issue when no one is around to assist you or you may share the information with someone else in need.

Next time you feel tired and overwhelmed, ask for the necessary and deserved help. Ask despite your anxieties and with an eye on the benefits. This might supply you with much more than simply the help you require.

Why Is It So Difficult to Request Help?

We would do much more, have more fun doing it, and experience the thrill of teamwork if we asked for help. Then why is it so challenging?

Our culture teaches that asking for help is a sign of weakness, so not surprisingly, our parents absorbed this belief and passed it on to us, maybe never challenging its validity or logic.

Most of us were raised with "family mantras" constantly playing in our heads until they became a part of us. Do not disturb the neighbors! If you want something done well, do it yourself! As we left for college, we honed our skills by listening to them, possibly the final words said to us.

Have you heard the story of the new bridegroom who wondered why his wife cut the end off the ham before cooking it? "Because my mum did," she said. When he had the chance, he asked her mother, and she responded, "Because my mother did."

The opportunity finally arose for him to inquire about this with his wife's grandma as he was eager to find out the truth. "Why did you cut the ham's end off before cooking it?" he inquired.

"Because my skillet was too small!" Three generations had never questioned the same habit.

Does it make sense to change this old attitude that it is a sign of weakness to seek help, and, if so, how? If you do not seek help, you do everything independently. This indicates that you are a busy person constantly receiving new demands in today's environment.

It also indicates that you have become achievement-oriented because your success has grown dependent on how effectively you handle everything on your own. What an elaborate trap! You have unknowingly adopted a highly severe lifestyle, which increases the likelihood you will experience stress-related side effects.

Then how does one alter the belief? It is simple to say, but it will take commitment and dedication to a new lifestyle to make it a reality. Your new belief might state, "Asking for help is a sign of strength!" As in the past, your behavior must follow your beliefs.

How will you behave after adopting this new belief? Science suggests that if you "act as if" you hold the new viewpoint; even though such transformations do not occur overnight, you will eventually embrace it after a period of acting it out.

Seek help when the time comes. At first, it will unsettle because you are accustomed to having complete control and will find it hard to relinquish some of it. Therefore, let's consider retaining some control by "languaging" your request. *The biggest thing I ever learned is that people support what they help build, so:*

❖ When would it be easier for you to demonstrate how you created this Excel spreadsheet?

❖ Is there a better time to help me lift this large piece of furniture?

❖ Let's devise a plan to tidy the house so we can go to the movies.

❖ Could you assist with the final phase of this project if I assist with the setup?

Each example includes the other person developing a strategy to make supporting you successful. The likelihood of outright rejection is reduced. A sense of togetherness accompanies the lack of complete control. That's a win-win situation.

When you believe it is a strength to ask for help, your self-esteem increases each time you do so, and someone agrees. We must balance this, just as with any other activity.

Your life becomes more balanced, so you experience less stress and have more time for interpersonal connections.

You observe that, because of everyone working together, overall production increases and morale improves.

What if I told you the belief that "asking for help is a strength" directly affects the bottom line? The power of one's convictions cannot be understated. They dictate our actions. We need to get to work if we want to act more equably, enjoy ourselves more, be more content, and see ourselves as a part of something much more significant than ourselves. We need to change a long-held belief about asking for aid!

Keys to Asking for Help

However, when you ask for help, you cede some power to another person, which can be frightening.

What if you are rejected?

They may believe you are stupid or that you should have worked it out on your own. Who wants to take that chance? It is easier to do everything by yourself, or is it?

Be able to envision being STUCK. If you are self-sufficient, you have taken the strength of self-sufficiency too far and become weak—isolating you, causing you stress, and making you responsible for everyone and everything with no backup or support. You have mastered the art of self-sufficiency and cannot go to the next stage of human development, which is interdependence.

Acknowledge that enough is enough. How would you behave if you believed that requesting help is a sign of strength? That asking is a form of generosity, allowing another person the honor of assisting you? That perhaps there is something more significant than every achievement being exceptional? Maybe you COULD examine each circumstance regarding whether asking for help will strengthen a connection. Perhaps do something mediocre if it means feeling part of something or belonging.

Simply do it. You might be terrified. Ambrose Redmon states, "Courage is not the absence of fear; it is determining that something else is more important than the dread." Start by asking a close, trustworthy friend or seek help in a field in which you excel. It is simpler or engages the person in planning how and when the "help" will occur.

Consequently, you will lose less control. "When would you be available to demonstrate how you created that spreadsheet?" It also reduces the likelihood of rejection. After some repetition and practice, you will wonder how you ever lived any other way. It is in equilibrium, liberating, more productive, and much more enjoyable!

CHAPTER 17
HIGHLY
PRODUCTIVE TEENS

Productivity has a different meaning for everyone. You practice enhancing your skills and knowledge when you set out to do something constructive. From helping your mother to cook to reading some social skills book, from enrolling in some computer diploma courses to joining summer camps or completing an internship, all are useful and productive things to engage in. But you must have a plan.

Create goals: Don›t feel bored or think it is too early to think about your future. Contemplate your hobbies, interests, and passion, and ponder what prospective career you can join. When you list your goals, it makes it easy to choose your next step.

Be Curious: You can come across learning to do various stuff just by reading about it. You have wanted to learn how to use a tool in specific software or learn some innovative things. Anything can be found and studied in a book.

Experiment: Teenage is a great time to experiment with many things so that by the time you turn an adult, you know yourself well and realize your strengths and weaknesses.

For instance, if you aspire to become a radio jockey but cannot communicate your thoughts suitably, this is a perfect time to change your desire or modify your abilities to meet your aims.

Connect with your parents: It is fundamental in any person›s life to connect with their parents, grandparents, cousins, or friends. You need their advice, support, and love. It makes you feel refreshed when you discover about your childhood from your parents or grandparents when you get along with your friends and discuss everything happening in your life.

Leadership

Now, let's talk about being productive on another level. We can all agree that leadership is essential for successful adults, but they were not always successful. Some started to lead as a teen, just like you. I remember people around my dad envying him because he held several degrees and businesses, was well known, and led by example. But, most of all, he was loved, not feared. He was a servant first. My dad always told me that to become a good leader, I had to learn how to serve. I had no clue what he insinuated.

Many doors were opened for me because I had the gut to accept an assistant lead position in a teen's leadership program; I had no skills. How hard could that be? Right? Skills can be learned. So, I did just that. I learned from the most experienced teacher I observed; I took notes, asked questions, and improved. Then I became the program leader, for seven years I have trained, and learned from many others. Simple, isn't it? Wrong, it wasn't simple, it took a lot of discipline, patience, accountability, and humility. It's not every day that those teenagers made my life worth fighting for. Ha-ha. Even if you are not in a leadership role, leadership skills are still helpful because they inspire others to succeed, ensure goals are accomplished, reduce conflict, and build connections with others. Every person can be a leader, whether at home, in the community, or at school.

Teen leadership entails the acquisition of numerous sorts of leadership abilities. In this example, Chris acquires three crucial leadership qualities as he takes three crucial steps toward organizing her dream vacation.

Chris desires a memorable summer vacation this year. His parents have entrusted him with some vacation planning responsibilities, and he enjoys spending time with his family and close friends. So, he imagines what he wants to occur over his summer vacation.

Step 1: Vision

A vision is a dream for the future, yet it should be expressed in the present tense as if it were currently taking place. It is the desired state of affairs you want to achieve after completing your tasks. A vision should be pleasant and provide an illustrative image.

Step 2: Objective

Your mission is what you will do to accomplish your vision. It consists of a declaration describing the steps necessary to achieve the objective. For example, some use a vision board and display realistic, achievable, and timed goals. Although the vision cannot be touched, displaying it provides some sustenance that can lead it to reality. It is clear guidance to realizing your vision.

Step 3: Planning and Setting Goals

Planning entails setting specific objectives and the action steps required to complete the task. Each brings you closer to successfully completing your purpose and, consequently, your vision. *The following are Chris's action steps for the previously stated mission:*

❖ Internet research of Caribbean destinations

❖ Discuss his research findings with his parents

❖ Research fun activities

❖ Book a hotel

❖ Schedule diving instruction

❖ Purchase beach wear and accessories

Now Chris truly has a detailed plan for reaching his destination.

Therefore, all he needs to do to achieve his ideal vacation is carry out his objective and plan as much as possible. Then he can go scuba diving in the Caribbean.

Briefly, your vision illustrates where you want to go; your mission provides a broad overview of how to get there, and your plan defines the objectives or steps you must take to attain your target.

Vision, mission, and strategy are necessary for adolescents aspiring to become influential youth leaders. Leadership abilities are most effectively acquired in a group context, such as in student leadership classes, which may be easily incorporated into every junior high and high school curriculum. You can gain knowledge from one another as you practice leadership skills. This structured group approach to leadership development will produce the best results for adolescents interested in becoming leaders.

Self Esteem and Self-Improvement

Self-esteem is a measure of how one feels about themselves. Low self-esteem indicates that you detest yourself due to your appearance, behavior, environment, or feelings. High self-esteem does not mean arrogance or believing you are superior to others. Self-respect implies having a positive relationship with who you are and loving and respecting yourself despite your imperfections. How does this relate to leadership?

Low self-esteem in leadership often leads to the need for a leader to micromanage their team. This is because they fear failure so much that they try to take on all the work themselves. They don't trust their team, so they convince themselves that micromanaging is the only way. When things go wrong, take the time to pick out the lessons within the experience. There will always be some to find. You need to use failure as a means of improvement rather than using it to beat yourself up. We build self-esteem by failing and learning, as well as succeeding.

You can build self-esteem by stepping out of your comfort zone. One of the best ways to improve your self-esteem is to step out of your comfort zone. Let yourself have the chance to fail. Do something hard or uncomfortable. If you fail, that's OK because sometimes we don't succeed at challenging tasks. But if you succeed, well, that's a different matter. Succeeding in something onerous or persevering through hardship is a great experience because you can refer to it later. There is nothing better in times of trouble to say to yourself: "Well, I did a similar thing before, and I came through it. I can do it again."

Have you ever seen a leader who always feels the need to be right? These leaders will often take good ideas from their teams and pass them off as their own. They don't like to be seen as wrong because this is a sign of *weakness.* They feel that because they are the leader, they need to be the strongest in the team at all things. But what about self-improvement?

Regardless of being a leader or not, we all have things we'd like to change about ourselves. And every leader knows you must constantly adapt and improve to achieve greatness.

Whatever you're working toward, it's essential to constantly assess, evaluate, and appraise where you are and want to be for the sake of those who are loyal to you and work hard to achieve your vision and goals. Great leaders make self-improvement a daily practice. Here are some examples of how to go about it:

They assess themselves honestly: To improve, you must acknowledge that you need improvement. Notice how you behave in different situations and see how it affects your team. You can't be a better leader if you don't acknowledge what you lack.

They educate themselves continually: Unsurprisingly, many leaders are avid readers. There is so much to learn and understand, and reading a book is like having the best teachers and the most brilliant mentors from history on demand.

They welcome feedback approvingly: They understand that feedback is a gift, and they seek critique from trusted people who can get straight to the point. Constructive feedback is the best way to learn how to improve.

They work toward their goals daily: Make it a habit to work toward a goal consistently, and every time you meet that goal, you'll learn more about yourself and discover more ways to self-improve.

They ask for support frequently: Top leaders know the benefits of having good counsel and intelligent advocates, and even the best leaders may have a coach.

Lead from within: In leadership, it's not about who you used to be but about who you choose to become.

Deal with your emotions

Adolescents naturally go through periods of intense emotion because their hormones are readjusting for adulthood and partly because they are experiencing things from a new viewpoint. New problems, new settings, and connections leave them bewildered and overwhelmed and can even drive them to withdraw, become fearful, and grow furious. This formerly carefree and joyful child you used to be may become someone hardly recognizable.

Adults also can experience moodiness. Shhhhh...Suppose they don't resolve or release emotions successfully when they first encounter them. There, they will take up residence in our minds or bodies and cause them to feel stressed, anxious, and angry, amplifying future emotions and stressful situations.

Part of the problem why is that no one taught you how to deal with and express emotions. It's not a class they teach at school, and since many adults have never learned techniques to release emotions constructively, they are not able to coach their children. This generates pressure in relationships and can further undermine self-worth—both for the teen and the parents.

Some everyday emotions teens experience are anxiety, frustration, shame, wrath, and exposure. This basic exercise is fast, straightforward, and effective no matter what has been troubling you. Give it a try!

First, you will want to pick a spot and time where you won't be bothered for a few minutes. You'll want to be able to focus as much as possible, so avoid as much distraction as you can. Now mentally, build a list of the things bugging you.

Listen to your inner intellect; listen to your heart. It doesn't matter if you agree with what comes up; notice any feelings boiling under the surface. Close your eyes.

Imagine each issue or feeling fills your body; then envision blowing all that emotion into a balloon. Exhale the emotion from your body and your mind. As you blow the emotion into the balloon, you may see that its color changes.

It may turn brown or black due to the negative emotion's energy. Imagine tying the balloon when it is full and releasing it into the sky. Continue filling, binding, and releasing the balloons until you experience complete relief. Allow yourself to feel at ease.

Then look up at the sky; it is filled with your negativity as those old balloons float through it. Imagine that they combine to form a large, dark cloud and realize that you have projected all your previous negative emotions into this cloud.

Now, if you are able, forgive all the people and situations that led you to feel so badly—forgive everyone involved, even if it's a tiny bit. Forgive them. Realize that holding on to rage and resentment does nothing but harm you.

Pardon yourself. Consider all the times you've made errors, misbehaved, or felt embarrassment or shame, and forgive yourself. Imagine the sun's emergence as you look up into the sky. Bright, pleasant, and reassuring, it emerges and disperses the shroud of negativity. Let it be dissolved. Just let it go.

As the veil of negativity dissipates, feel the sun's warmth trickling into your body, enveloping each cell with peace, comfort, warmth, and love. Allow yourself to feel accepted and appreciated. Reassure yourself that you are fine.

Now, attempt to identify something about you that you value. Perhaps you have shown kindness to someone. Maybe you possess a particular knack or skill. Perhaps you can appreciate yourself for your strength, love of animals, love of people, brilliance, sense of humor, silliness, or spirit; find something. Enjoy this aspect of yourself. You are good and believe that within. Believe it, value yourself for it, and accept yourself.

Applying your creativity with this technique is acceptable—make the balloons different colors and imagine inflating them so much they burst and splatter.

Consistent use of this technique will assist you in balancing your emotions, releasing the daily negativity you encounter, and enhancing your self-esteem while dealing with your emotions.

CHAPTER 18
SOCIAL SKILLS FOR A BETTER YOU

Individual personality qualities colored by different environmental influences play a significant part in deciding who achieves life success. It includes social variables such as experience, reputation, and qualifications. Unique talents and skills derived from social capital, such as personal contacts, become crucial to an individual's success.

While technology seems to have diminished our potential for direct person-to-person contact, it is about connection. *Regardless, let's analyze the six social abilities for success in all sectors.*

1. Social Networking

Embrace or establish a social network. To expand, social skill activities require communities. Through networks, information is more accessible; more individuals equal more information, and more people with more knowledge generate leverage, trust, and power.

2. Take the Initiative and Be Deliberate:

Successful individuals are dedicated, innovative, and adaptable. They take the initiative to be social, display a willingness to learn, and possess exceptional analytical abilities. Take responsibility for improving your soft skills by honing your communication abilities and improving your ability to manage stress, whether self-inflicted or externally imposed.

3. Mutual Respect

The Golden Rule transcends time:

⬩　Treat people as you would like to be treated.

⬩　Increase your ability to demonstrate tolerance and mutual respect and provide and accept criticism.

⬩　Exhibit genuine praise and gratitude when something positive occurs for another individual.

Genuinely praising others is an indication of self-assurance. Taking the time to celebrate someone else's accomplishment is infectious and complimentary.

4. Listen more, Speak Less

The gift of gab is not necessarily a characteristic of those who appear to be natural achievers. These individuals are typically excellent with others since they are excellent listeners. This quality can be cultivated to great advantage. It is simple to demonstrate a genuine interest in others by asking questions and speaking less. The ability to listen is a social skill that will improve your relationships with other individuals. People naturally prefer to converse. Therefore, you can distinguish yourself by practicing active listening.

5. Maintain Eye Contact

Have you ever chatted with a friend preoccupied with his smartphone or simply looking away? For example, a teenager was recently invited to a summer camp job interview but only made eye contact with her prospective employer twice during the interview. Despite her skills and academic achievements, she was let go because her behavior reflected a lack of respect for her potential employer. This summer camp jamb would have been good for her resume, showing innovation and ambitions at such a young age can open so many doors you wouldn't even have thought possible.

The source of distraction was her cell phone. "The New Rude" refers to avoiding eye contact or succumbing to simple distractions in social situations. Personal interaction is an outward manifestation of attention, respect, and involvement. Also, it is a defining characteristic of outstanding leaders since they thrive on information to make informed decisions.

6. Be Observant and Attentive to Specifics

The enormous pressure of current times has led to many adopting a false sense of security, which gives the external appearance that everything is okay. Certainly not, we all have a life outside of school, jobs, and shopping malls. Only the most observant individuals can identify the difference between your parent's or friend's facial expression or body language alteration. This can provide more insight into tackling the situation, which can be a relationship-defining moment.

Acquiring and mastering these social skills will enable you to have an infectious personality and succeed in life. Focus more on speaking less and being more observant. Ask the right questions and it will be easy for others to connect with you. A certain level of social awareness is required to navigate the social sphere. Adulthood does not mark the end of social skills development. You are continually learning and adjusting, even subconsciously, no matter your age.

But teens lack the life experiences of adults and rarely comprehend why they must see, do or say things they do not wish to. Even some adults with a great deal of sophistication do not fully comprehend how social etiquette has evolved over the past decade. For instance, are there specific hours and locations where you may use your phone? How do you communicate in a multi-media environment?

However, there are three certainties regarding developing and maintaining social skills:

1. Seeing

Seeing involves identifying social cues. Consider the situation's setting. Is it formal or casual?

Are the individuals you interact with acquaintances, strangers, or casual friends? Different circumstances call for varied behaviors.

When social seeing, one must exercise sound judgment. Observe the behavior of the individuals around you and their responses to different events. Essentially, social seeing is subtly avoiding incorrect acts or responses.

2. Reflecting

The second of these social skill fundamentals entails evaluating the actions of others and comprehending their motivations. In addition, it involves anticipating possible responses and devising effective means of dealing with a problem or individual.

When you misinterpret others' intentions and cannot immediately come up with constructive solutions to social problems, it is highly indicative you have social difficulties.

3. Doing

This is about interacting positively with others. Often, we are aware of what we ought to do but have difficulties carrying it out. For instance, we may wish to join a discussion group yet freeze and experience anxiety in the social environment of the scenario. We are highly self-conscious or completely ashamed. If you lack social awareness, you may also speak rashly. It is essential to at least initiate or join a conversation.

These three social skill fundamentals are necessary for developing and maintaining all social abilities. An enthusiastic and boisterous approach may not be the greatest method to address a situation that calls for quiet decorum. Social skills involve adapting your conduct and being adaptable in any circumstance. Different definitions exist for social skills, but they are the capacity to get along with others and maintain satisfying relationships.

CONCLUSION

Most teenagers are growing up disconnected in a world not built for face-to-face communication. But don't let that be you! Social abilities are typically the most critical skills a person can possess as they often serve as predictors of success. Man is a sociable animal, and a life of loneliness is inevitable if social skills are inadequate. No man is an island but making friends can be a challenge if you lack social skills. Teenagers with well-developed social skills are likely to gain confidence in their abilities to approach situations and complete tasks more successfully. Peer rejection, bullying, conflict, social isolation, depression, anger, anxiety, and poor academic performance may all be signs of poor social skills. Anyone can build abilities, and it does not require specialized instruction. The most significant aspect of increasing social skills is the requirement for extensive practice. They are solid talents that can help you establish friends and obtain a good job, allowing you to achieve essential life advancements.

After learning everything there is to know about the growth of social skills, it is time to exercise them. Even though it's challenging to practice something you are not particularly good at, you will need to do so. Using these general rules, you can go step by step, at your own pace, until you have it all figured out. Rome wasn't created in a day, and neither can your social skills be improved overnight. You must be patient and composed. Know that you are not alone. Come on now, get to it. But don't worry, you got this!!!

Best wishes,

PLEASE LEAVE A REVIEW

As an independent author, reviews are my livelihood on this platform. SCAN THE QR CODE TO LEAVE A REVIEW ☺

ALSO, FROM THIS AUTHOR

UPCOMING RELEASES

AUTHOR BIO

With a professional background in healthcare and a passion for helping others unleash their true potential, Wildine's writing is warm and refreshingly honest. She is an advocate for living the life you want to live, speaking things into existence, and finding your purpose on earth.

As the author of **Highly Effective Teens With MAD Social Skills,** Wildine hopes to empower the next generation, blending her cordial writing style with her years spent researching psychology and mental health. She aims to inspire teens with the tools they need to thrive emotionally, socially, and academically. She understands the thought process, the power of the mental attitude, emotional resilience, assertiveness, and boundary-setting in the modern world. Her willingness to share personal stories from her own life, with her straightforward and focused advice, makes it easy for readers to implement changes immediately. When she's not writing or focusing on helping others, you might find her traveling the world, catching on her favorite shows, running a marathon, or playing candy crush.

Wildine speaks fluently (French, Creole, English) and Spanish moderately. Wildine currently resides in northern California with her supportive husband, two beautiful sons, and a pair of overactive huskies.

REFERENCES

Ann V. (1986). Perceptions of peer pressure, peer conformity dispositions, and self-reported behavior among adolescents, *Developmental Psychology, 22*:4, 521–530.

Avery, A. W., Rider, K., & Haynes-Clements, L. A. (1981). Communication skills training for adolescents: A five-month follow-up. *Adolescence, 16*(62), 289–298.

Bagwell, C. L., & Schmidt, M. E. (2011). Friendships in Childhood.

Banu, Saira, Daragad, M. & Venkat Lakshmi. H. (2013). Social Skills and Behavior of School Children In Dharwad District. IOSR Journal of Humanities and Social Science, 14(3), 49–51.

Barber, B. K., & Erickson, L. D. (2001). Adolescent social initiative: Antecedents in the ecology of social connections. Journal of Adolescent Research, 16(4), 326–354.

Bath, C. (2009). Learning to Belong: Exploring Young Children's Company they Keep, edited by W. M. Bukowski., A. F. Newcomb., and WW. Hartup. 1–15.

Bender, D., & Loesel, F. (1997). Protective and risk effects of peer relations and social support on antisocial behavior in adolescents from multi-problem milieus. *Journal of Adolescence, 20*(6), 661–678.

Brown B. B. (2004). Adolescents' relationships with peers. In R. M. Lerner & L. Steinberg (Eds.), Handbook of Adolescent Psychology, 2nd edition (pp. 363–394). New York: Wiley.

Burleson, B. R. (2010). The nature of interpersonal communication. The Handbook of Communication Science (pp.145–163).

Cranor, C. (1975). Toward a Theory of Respect for Persons.

D'Souza, A. (2005). Why You Need Social Skills. Source: rediff.com

Dunn, J. (2004). Children's Friendships: The Beginnings of Intimacy. Oxford: Blackwell Publishing.

Fink, C.F. Some conceptual difficulties in the theory of social conflict. Journal of Conflict Resolution, 1968, 12(4), 412–460.

Fisher, R.J. (1990) Third party consultation: A method for the study and resolution of conflict. *Journal of Conflict Resolution,* 1972, 16, 67–94.

Fisher, R.J. (1990) The social psychology of intergroup and international conflict resolution. New York: Springer-Verlag.

Galanaki, E. P., & Kalantzi-Azizi, A. (1999). Loneliness and social dissatisfaction: Its relationship with children's self-efficacy for peer interaction. *Child Study Journal, 29*(1), 1–22.

Guthrie, I. K. (1999). Contemporaneous and longitudinal relations of dispositional sympathy to emotionality, regulation, and social functioning. *Journal of Early Adolescence, 19*(1), 66–97.

Hargie, O. (2010). Communicating effectively: The skills approach. In O. Hargie (Ed.), Skilled interpersonal communication: Research, theory and practice (5th ed., pp. 1–12). New York

Haun, Daniel B. M.; Tomasello, Michael (2011). "Conformity to Peer Pressure in Preschool Children". *Child Development 82* (6): 1759 1767. ISSN 1467-8624.

Haven, CT (1975). Yale University Press. Deutsch, M. and Coleman, P. (eds.). The Handbook of Conflict Resolution: Theory and practice. San Francisco: Jossey-Bass, 2000.

Kaplan, Leslie S. Coping with Peer Pressure. New York: Hazelden/ Rosen (1997). A book for young adults   that offers suggestions on how to keep peer pressure from controlling your life.

Matsumoto, D. (2010). APA handbook of interpersonal communication (pp. ix–xiv). New York City: American Psychological Association.

Openshaw, D. K., Mills, T. A., Adams, G. R., & Durso, D. D. (1992). Conflict resolution in parent-adolescent dyads.

Puccinelli, N. M. (2010). Nonverbal communicative competence. In D. Matsumoto (Ed.), APA Handbook of Interpersonal Communication (pp. 273–288). New York City

Sabee, C. M. (2015). Interpersonal communication skill/competence. In The International Encyclopedia of Interpersonal Communication (pp. 1–9). Hoboken, NJ, USA: John Wiley & Sons, Inc. https://doi.org/10.1002/9781118540190.wbeic080

Sharma, Reetu, Goswami, Vandana & Gupta, Purnima (2016). Social Skills: Their Impact on

Academic Achievement and other Aspects of Life.